Ready, Set, Growth Hack: A Beginner's Guide to Growth Hacking Success

Ready, Set, Growth Hack: A Beginner's Guide to Growth Hacking Success

Nader Sabry

Ordering information: Special discounts are available on quantity purchases by governments, NGOs, schools, companies, associations, and others. For details, contact the publisher at www.ReadySetGrowthHack.com or www.nadersabry.com.

Printed in the United States of America and Canada.

Nader Sabry, *Ready, Set, Growth hack:*
A beginners guide to growth hacking success

Ebook ISBN 978-1-9163569-0-0
Paperback ISBN 978-1-9163569-1-7
Hardcover ISBN 978-1-9163569-2-4
Audiobook ISBN 978-1-9163569-3-1

1. BUSINESS & ECONOMICS / Entrepreneurship, 2. BUSINESS & ECONOMICS / Corporate Finance / Venture Capital, 3. BUSINESS & ECONOMICS / Industries / Computers & Information Technology

First Edition, and first print in 2020

Nader Sabry
Royal Oak. P.O. Box 91022
Calgary Alberta, Canada T3G 0B1

www.ReadySetGrowthHack.com

CONTENTS

FIGURES

Exercises

Preface

For two and a half decades, I have being building startups, growing corporates, and advancing governments. As a strategist, I can sit back and carefully analyze what makes an organization work or not work. With extreme fascination, I have found a few core elements that have significant impact.

These elements are based on their mindset, and how much value they put into growth. When I say growth, I don't mean marketing and sales. I mean holistically accounting for everything, but starting with the mindset itself. Founders, CEOs, and government leaders who are growth focused would see better results nine out of ten times.

What make those leaders different have been their levels of clarity and focus? In turn, this clarity and focus align with a very keen eye on execution, with an openness and flexibility for experimenting with new ideas and processes. These successful leaders started by understand they did not necessarily know the answers, but had to find solutions quickly that would directly impact growth — everything else would follow.

These observations along with my experience starting several of my own companies led me to write this book, which is aimed at helping those who are starting or running an existing a business, whether small or large. It will also help government leaders commissioned with a growth mandate.

From start to finish, this book will help those who want a disproportionate form of growth get started with their first growth hack, then replicate it over and over again, sustaining scalable growth in their own organizations.

LET'S GET GROWING!

Chapter 1.
Introduction: why do companies need to growth hack?

David and Goliath: Defeating the Giant

Growth hacking is a shortcut to growth that enables the weak to defeat the strong. As a way of an example, we all know the story of David and Goliath. In fact, we know many stories like it: the smaller, weaker opponent triumphs over the stronger rival. But why are there so many instances of this being the case?

In his book *David and Goliath,* Malcolm Gladwell quotes the research of political scientist Ivan Arreguín-Toft, who wanted to find out just how often the underdog wins. Arreguín-Toft analyzed every war fought in the last two hundred years where there was a big difference in the strength or size of the participants. In most cases, the larger army won. But the split wasn't what you'd think. In fact, in almost 30% of cases, the smaller army triumphed over its more powerful enemy (Figure 1).

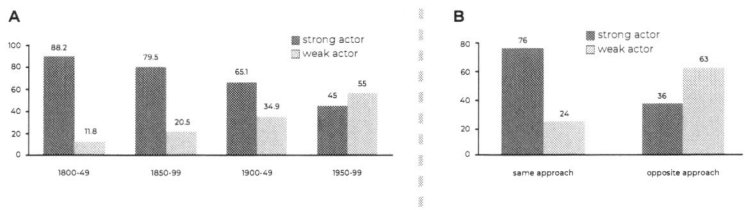

Figure 1. How the weak win in war

Smaller Armies Play by Their Own Rules

What is it about small armies that make them punch above their weight? Further analysis gave Arreguín-Toft a clue. When he looked at the tactics employed by the smaller armies, he saw that they often adopted unconventional strategies like guerilla warfare to make up for their lack of physical strength. Using different strategies often changed the results. According to Arreguín-Toft's research, when smaller armies thought outside the box, they beat their opponents a whopping 63% of the time (Figure 1).

Why the weak win

When evaluating war mechanics and understanding why the weak win, you will find three main elements. First, they change their tactics dynamically; second, they adjust quickly to changes; and, third, they are willing to take bold actions. The tactics taken are decisive due to smaller decision-making layers, rapid flow of intelligence, and cultivation of a victorious attitude towards winning. The adjustments form a decisive mechanism that allows intelligence to turn into action quickly, within a relevant timeframe, and within context of change. Finally, bold actions can be taken when tactics and adjustments align quickly and effectively — immediately enabling bold actions taken by the leadership. Furthermore, all of these elements don't even start to account for exploitation of technology.

When the underdogs played by their own rules and acknowledged their strengths, they became the favorites.

Leverage War Mechanics for Growth

It isn't something new when a weaker part wins over a stronger one, but the question remains how this happens. It is important to point out that this upset occurs across all applications, whether it is a personal adversary in politics, a competitor in business, or a war between military or even organized crime groups.

The fundamental principle of war mechanics is to change patterns that are usually governed by rules that are set and enforced by stronger opponents. This very fact that they have set the rules is ironically where their weakness stem, enabling weaker players to flip stronger opponents.

HOW GROWTH HACKING CAME INTO EXISTENCE
EVOLUTIONARY BREAKDOWN OF WHERE
GROWTH HACKING REALLY ORIGINATES

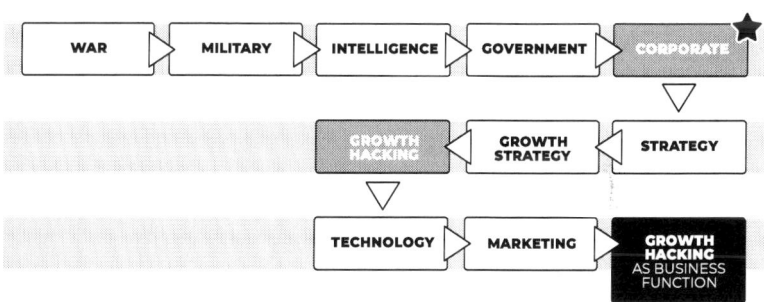

Figure 2. How growth hacking came into existence

Before discussing war mechanics more fully, it's important to understand its relationship with growth hacking. When you break down the evolutionary path, you can see that growth hacking is about war mechanics (Figure 2). The reason is that growth hacking solves for

- Weaker parties beating strong ones;
- Using less effort to gain disproportionate results;

- Effectively optimized use of resources; and
- Creative measures not previously used or not used in the same way as before.

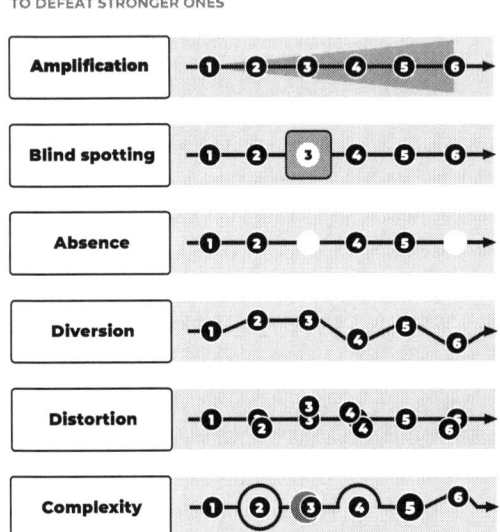

Figure 3. Six types of warfare mechanics

Six broad mechanics can be leveraged to change the rules and defeat your opponent (Figure 3). These mechanics can be virtual, physical, or a blend of the two using deep psychology, strategic shifts, precision operations, and tactical movements.

Amplification. Increase the volume of misleading information creating confusion and miscalculated responses by your opponents. This approach will waste your opponent's resources and distorting their plans.

- Bigger than life — magnifying movements (or the lack of movement)
- Speeding up — showing an intensified increase in speed
- Perceived advancements — wins that are neither calculated nor seen

Blind spotting. Immediate or emerging weaknesses that have not been used against the opponent before — at all or not well enough — can be exploited. These gaps indicate positions the opponent has not covered well.

- Known — blind spots that the opponent is not competently fixing
- Unknown — blind spots of which the opponent is not aware
- Created —new blind spots created for your opponent

Absence. By removing parts that your opponent is focused on in order to divert attention to other places, you can leave them confused while spending time guessing your next moves.

1. Known — points your opponent is focused on to use against you
2. Unknown — faking absence in areas that your opponent believes exist
3. Created — pitfalls that lead your opponent into wasting time and resources

Diversion. You can manipulate your opponent's perception by creating new rules, information, and circumstances that may exist but are diverted. Creating complex new situations can lead to your opponents wasting their resources.

1. Enemies — creating new ones or partnering with existing ones to intensify efforts

2. Spin —confusing opponents and those working with and around them
3. Redirect — changes to make weakness seemingly appear where they don't actually exist

Distortion. Falsify information, the role of players, and changes in conditions and circumstances in order to influence others around your opponent and within your opponent's organization.

1. Information — manipulate information to confuse opponent and their network
2. Actions — manipulate actions, whether real or fake, to reshape circumstances
3. Relationships — transform how the players involved are aligned

Complexity. Create or reconfigure elements to create more complexity, making it harder for your opponents to decode your thinking and planned actions, and overwhelming them into bad decisions.

1. New — obstacles that did not exist are created to drive confusion
2. Adjustment — leverage existing obstacles to drive confusion
3. Shift — divert attention to underutilized obstacles to drive confusion

These mechanics are applicable across many situations. They enable you to leverage the patterns created through the mechanics used in warfare. Warfare-like sports are an easy playbook to understand because they have two opposing positions with a single winner as the outcome. The complexity is in how to win, not just in the playbook structure itself.

How Do Underdogs Win?

Through your business, you might find yourself as the underdog in your industry. Other larger companies dominate the market, making it difficult for you to make yourself heard. In many industries, a handful of companies own the vast majority of market share. In the UK media, for example, a recent study by Media Reform Coalition showed that just five companies controlled over 80% of the national newspaper market.

WHAT HELPS THE UNDERDOGS WIN

THESE FIVE STRATEGIES ARE USED BY WEAKER OPPONENTS TO WIN AGAINST STRONGER CONTENDERS

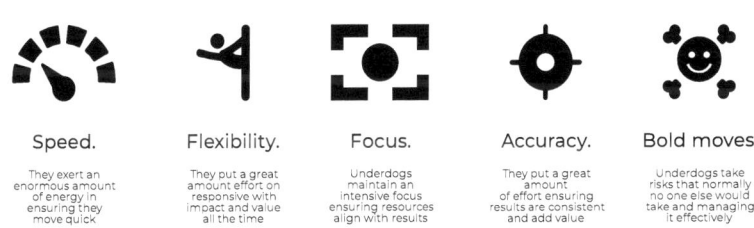

Speed.	Flexibility.	Focus.	Accuracy.	Bold moves.
They exert an enormous amount of energy in ensuring they move quick	They put a great amount effort on responsive with impact and value all the time	Underdogs maintain an intensive focus ensuring resources align with results	They put a great amount of effort ensuring results are consistent and add value	Underdogs take risks that normally no one else would take and managing it effectively

Figure 4. The five strategies that help underdogs win

So how can you compete with the industry leaders?

Warfare and underdog strategies

When a weaker opponent decides to apply a warfare mechanic, it will choose either a single direction or multiple strategic directions (Figure 5). For example, a weaker opponent might select an amplification mechanic through speed and flexibility (first line of Figure 5). This choice translates into using intensive approaches with speed to overwhelm and flexibility to exploit vulnerability that may have not been visible initially.

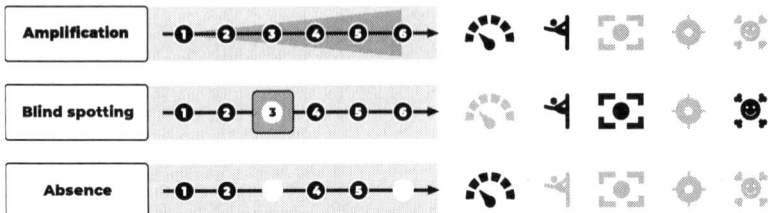

Figure 5. How underdogs apply warfare mechanics

Working through a few possibilities it is important to eva-luate the multitude of options that will best exploit your opponent. Figure 5 shows a few ways of applying multiple strategies (Lines 1 and 2) or even single ones (Line 3) like an absence mechanic with a speed strategy that creates total confusion and diversion.

Growth hackers use their weaker opponents to optimize their ability to win against strong opponents. The best of growth hacks initially avoid warfare all together. However, it is inevitable that, with time, competition will arise and a battle will break out.

Uber, Tinder, and PayPal

One company that found itself in an underdog position was Uber. Before the ridesharing service came about, the only way to request a ride anywhere was to call a taxi. Uber knew it had figured out a way to make trips more affordable and more accessible, but how could it grow the company to compete with regular taxi services?

In this instance, growth was defined by the number of downloads of the Uber app, as well as an increase in the number of drivers signing up for the service. The more people who used the service and the more drivers they recruited, the greater Uber's market share would be.

Thus, increasing those downloads and sign-ups was critical for Uber to succeed. If this kind of growth had not been in place, Uber would not have become the standard for ride-sharing around the world.

So how did they do it? Uber's founders decided to use their existing customers to find new ones. They'd send free rides to their friends and family in exchange for discounts. As more people signed up, they were encouraged to get others to join. The growth became exponential. Rather than relying on traditional marketing methods — like sending out email blasts or posting ads online — Uber used its own app as the primary source of its buzz.

Uber's not the only startup to achieve this level of growth from unconventional methods. Take Airbnb, an online marketplace offering lodging and tourism experiences. Its founders were able to build an extensive network of users in just a few years by piggybacking off of Craigslist — the existing platform for renting a room. By targeting the Craigslist consumer with an alternative, Airbnb went from 0.14 million to 40 million users in just five years.

The dating app Tinder is another example. Before 2013, meeting people was a chore. You had to create a profile, fill out a lengthy amount of information, and then hope that you found a match. But Tinder expedited this process, by introducing a "swipe" feature. By 2014, Tinder had 10 million users; by the end of that year, 40 million users were swiping one billion times a day.

Perhaps the most famous example of this different approach to marketing is PayPal. It's hard to imagine a time when the online payment giant didn't exist, but back in 2000 it was just an idea. An online method of secure payment that didn't require a credit card each time? The idea was novel. But PayPal's use of unconventional marketing was superb. By introducing a referral system where users could get real bonuses into their account, PayPal grew from 1 million users in March 2000 to 5 million users by July. Now that's hyper-growth.

How Do You Know When You Need Growth Hacking

If you are experiencing one or all of the following, then growth hacking is something you will want to explore seriously:

- Your competitors are gaining market share faster than you.
- New entrants are gaining more growth than you.
- You cannot keep up with the change in consumer needs.
- Traditional value-creation tactics are no longer successful.
- Sustaining profitable growth no longer works.
- Margins are getting squeezed.
- You face an increase in pressure to change operating models.
- Many attempts to grow have failed.
- Cost cutting is the only focus.

Not all organizations are ready for growth. They may need it, they may want it, and it might literally mean them shutting down, but they may not be ready. It is vital to ensure growth isn't realized too late.

What to Expect from Growth Hacking

Growth hacking can help you make the mechanics under the hood effective, efficient, and uniquely competitive so that you can become a new breed of growth machine. Specifically, growth hacking helps you:

- Develop a long view on growth that lets you see everything;
- Become future focused and future proof;
- Gain flexibility and become super-honed in responsiveness;
- Harness optimization to its extreme boundaries;
- Create unparalleled value in nontraditional ways;
- Become notoriously competitive; and
- Grow in profitability.

Although the end goal is growth, you are essentially building a well-oiled machine to sustain long-term prosperity, taking into account short-term opportunities with a long-term view on how to evolve competitively.

Barriers to Growth Hacking

A variety of barriers can prevent organizations from successful growth hacking, including the following:

- Lack of talent to drive growth;
- Processes to make growth work;
- Inflexible business models that restrict growth;
- Ineffective innovation that inhibits growth; and
- Capital constraints that keep you from funding growth.

Being aware of, acknowledging, and addressing these barriers will help you prepare so that you can find proper solutions. Growth hacking doesn't have to be a cumbersome or expensive exercise. It's quite the contrary. Growth hacking can be achieved with a small budget and a short time frame, while having a major impact.

Growth Hacking Works

What do companies like Uber, Tinder, and PayPal — which all achieved unprecedented levels of growth in a short time — have in common? They used a method of marketing called growth hacking.

In popular culture, the term *hack* has come to mean a shortcut in almost any area of life. Google "life hacks," "food hacks," or even "Ikea hacks" and you'll find websites dedicated to giving people quick, easy, and clever shortcuts to some of life's conundrums.

A hack can be anything that makes life easier, quicker, cheaper, or more effective. It's a strategy or technique for managing one's time or activities more efficiently. It's not just a shortcut; it's also a way of doing things that is out of the ordinary and yields magnified results. For example, Airbnb hacked its way to new customers via a platform they were already using; PayPal hacked its way by getting existing customers to find new ones. In both cases, the ultimate goal was to create explosive growth using any means possible.

And that's what growth hacking is all about: growth. According to the man who coined the term, Sean Ellis, a growth hacker is someone whose "true north" is growth. Simply put, it's a term that describes a company or marketer focused on a single goal: growing the brand.

Growth Hacking: The Facts

- Marketer Sean Ellis coined the term *Growth Hacking* in 2010. Ellis had run growth hacking marketing campaigns for file-sharing giant Dropbox and events site Eventbrite.
- Google runs 7000 growth hacking experiments a day. Amazon runs 2000, Netflix 1000, and Facebook over 100,000.
- LinkedIn now has a growth hacking team with over 120 members.
- Booking.com conducts 1,000 tests a day optimizing its platform by spending $3.5 billion a year on Pay Per Click (PPC) advertising.

The fact that these high-growth companies are investing in constant experimentation shows that growth hacking isn't just the latest buzzword. These companies want to find the most successful ways to market their brand — not to gain followers or other vanity metrics, but to *grow*.

Growth Hacking Enhances *Everything Else*

But isn't all business about growth? Surely anything that builds brand awareness or increases demand for a product or service is going to lead to growth? Well, yes and no. All too often, startups and companies get distracted by vanity metrics. Likes, shares, and subscribers look good on the surface, but if no one is buying your product, then what difference does it make? Growth hacking is more focused. It's a determined effort with one goal in mind: to achieve hyper-growth on a consumer level. And that means sales.

Most traditional marketing methods are about creating buzz. But growth hacking is about more than this. It's about turning interest into quantifiable numbers. While traditional marketers may try to get more site visits or subscribers to an email list, a growth hacker is concerned only with increasing the number of paying customers.

As you can imagine, these methods can go hand in hand. As a product or service gets more paying customers, buzz and awareness will be natural side effects. The best growth hacking doesn't work outside of traditional marketing, but it enhances everything else you do.

So How Does Growth Hacking Work?

No one starts a company without having a well-developed idea. Sure, you could jump in with both feet before you really understand what your company will be doing or offering, but that's just a recipe for disaster.

The same is true for growth hacking. Until you know the finer points of this methodology and how it can work, any attempt to apply it to your startup is going to be a crash course in failure. That's why this book is more than a step-by-step guide to growth hacking but also a practical and insightful guide on how to execute your first growth hack and keep repeating it with success.

You don't have to be a growth hacker

*It's important to know that you do not have to be an expert in this field, but you will need to understand how it works (Figure 6). This book is designed for those with **no-to-little expertise** or even those with no exposure to the topic. It will help them get started driving growth in their own organization — whether a startup, a corporation, or government.*

Figure 6. low barriers to entry into growth hacking

I'm going to help you prepare yourself to growth hack the right way. I'm going to get you ready, set, and then show you how to use this incredible method to reach long-term goals in half the time.

What will be covered is the mindset and tools needed, how to get ready, how to experiment, how to implement and scale growth hacks. Bonus chapters discuss how to hire a growth hacker, 50 proven growth hacks to draw on, and 88 tools to get you started.

CHAPTER NOTES

CHAPTER NOTES

Chapter 2.
Growth hacking mindset: create the right growth hacking mindset

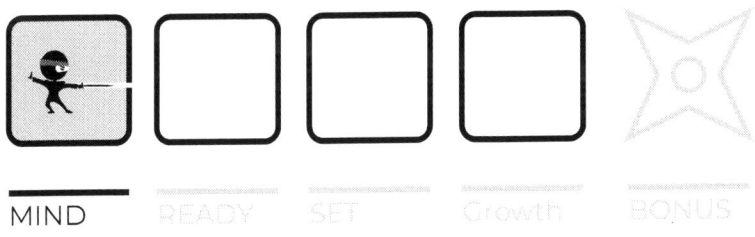

MIND — READY — SET — Growth — BONUS

In this chapter:

- the *three components* of successful growth hacking
- the *tools* available and their benefits
- *how to use* tools and make the most of them

> **KEY TAKEAWAY:**
> *To growth hack your way to success, you need to understand how growth hacking works. This understanding will enable you to choose and use the best tools — and people — for the job.*

Whenever you hear talk about marketing for a startup company, a number of buzzwords come up. *Digital transformation, disruption, beta testing, pivoting* — there doesn't seem to be an end to the list of things you *should* be doing. Is growth hacking just another buzzword?

Growth hacking isn't a bandwagon I'm inviting you to jump on. It's a genuine, purposeful, and practical way of achieving hyper-growth for your business. The purpose of this book is to help you understand the core components of growth hacking and get ready to employ them in your startup. I hope you'll see that growth hacking is not only nothing to be afraid of, but also a vital part of any startup's success.

I will illustrate the best ways to make growth hacking a part of your marketing strategy. But first we need to understand the theory and the tools behind growth hacking success.

What Is Growth Hacking?

Growth hacking is a shortcut to growth. It's about finding the most effective methods for growing your business in the shortest amount of time. A constant process of experimentation, multifunctional marketing, and data analysis allows us to find the methods that provide the most growth for the least amount of effort. I like to think of it as follows:

Growth hacking is the transformation point between four units of effort producing one unit of results and one unit of effort producing four units of results (Figure 7). — Nader Sabry

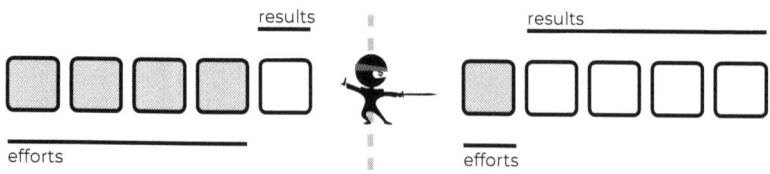

Figure 7. What is growth hacking

There are three keywords to remember when understanding the theory behind growth hacking: *experimentation*, *cross-functionality*, and *analytics*. These three components work together to make growth hacking effective.

Experimentation is the creative side of growth hacking. It's about coming up with new ideas for increasing revenue and trying them out to see what works (Figure 8). Without creativity, growth hacking has no fuel.

For example, TIMEZ5 Global Inc. founded a logistical hack by intentionally delaying their packages to the logistics providers on weekends to ensure quicker delivery the next morning. Another good example, WeTransfer.com provided creative wallpapers as advertisements while users spent time uploading their files on their website.

Experimentation

Running a series of structured and sequenced experiments to discover the outcome that best generates real results

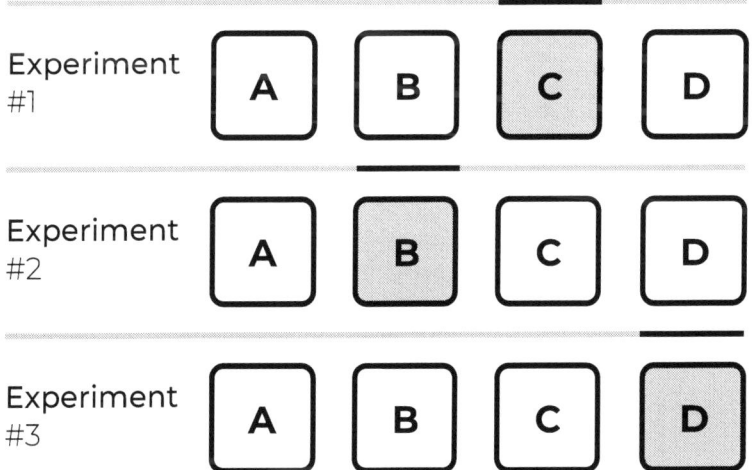

Figure 8. Structures of experimentations in growth hacking

Cross-functionality is the engine of the growth hacking machine. It's where technology, IT, marketing, and product delivery come together to make hyper-growth possible. In the past, growth hacking just involved hackers coming up with innovative ways to improve their code in order to promote sales. But the days of marketing strategies focusing on one area of expertise are gone. Coding experiments quickly evolved to include marketing tactics, especially in the area of digital marketing, from there, growth hacking quickly progressed again. Eventually, growth hackers realized that they could take a fully cross-functional approach that included product and service operations as well as marketing and code (Figure 9).

EVOLUTION OF GROWTH HACKING
Today's growth hacking has evolved from just code to a cross-functional approach

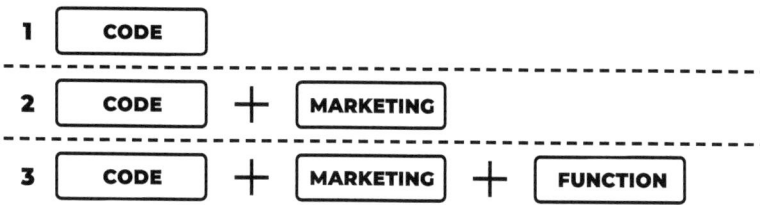

Figure 9. The evolution of growth hacking

Analytics is where growth hacking gets serious. By measuring the results of growth hacking experiments across all the different functions of a business, the process of growing that company becomes a science, not an art (Figure 10).

DATA ANALYTICS
Analyze and optimize cycles to qualify, disqualify, and discover data that enables growth

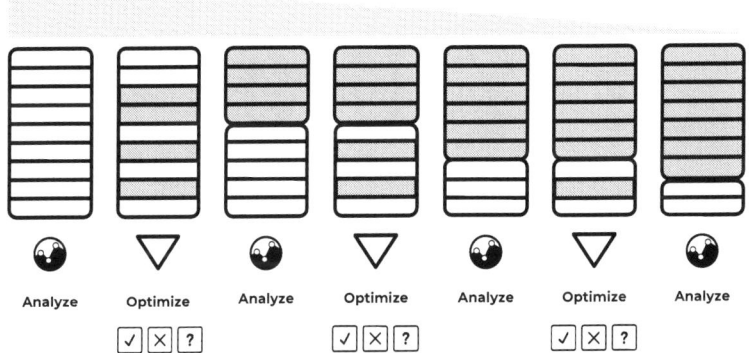

Figure 10. Data analytic optimization model

Experimentation

Technologist Aaron Ginn describes a growth hacker as having "a mindset of data, creativity, and curiosity." This curiosity is at the heart of growth hacking success. Trying out new methods and testing them to see what works is the fundamental job of a growth hacker. By doing so, we can find methods that lead to rapid and cost-effective hyper-growth.

Growth hacking is the point at which the relationship between your efforts and your results is transformed. It's a shortcut to growth. It's about taking an untried growth technique, testing it, learning from it, then scaling what works to maximize its utility. Experimentation is at the core of this process so that more and more growth hacks can be discovered.

It's important to note that growth hacking isn't isolated to digital methods. Although digital means are vital to making a growth hack work, growth hacking is not digital *per se*. Instead, I'd like you to think of any growth hack as having the following characteristics:

1. Fast — can be used to convert customers in a short amount of time
2. Cost effective — experiments don't require significant funding
3. Repeatable — can be repeated rapidly to deliver the same or better results
4. Flexible — can be adapted quickly and still maintain characteristics 1–3
5. Measurable — can be analyzed at a granular level to enable profound learning

Experimentation is key to find what growth hacks will work.

Cross-Functionality

In the beginning, growth hacking was built around a single function: coding. Growth hackers focused solely on finding clever ways to enhance their code to optimize their commercial outcomes, for example, automating routine processes to gain speed and accuracy.

Today, growth hacking has matured into a dual-function approach by bringing code and marketing together in a digital marketing context. Growth hacking has a narrow focus initially where only digital-oriented companies benefit. But the future of growth hacking is cross-functional, where both digital-based and non-digital-based companies can seize the opportunity of growth hacking. This is where code, marketing, and other business disciplines are integrated, influencing not just the front end of a business (marketing), but also the back end (product and service delivery).

This integration enhances customer experience and enables businesses to capitalize on cost-effective digital tools to supercharge their growth.

Technologist Andrew Chen summarized this point when he described the term *growth hacker* as "a hybrid of marketer and coder, who solves the question 'How do I get customers for my product?' by using A/B tests, landing pages, viral factors, email deliverability and Open Graphs." In short, there are many components of growth hacking. To achieve success, we need to use as many of them as we can. Here's how this holistic approach works.

Every organization — whether it's a startup, a corporation, or a government — does three things. It makes, it sells, and it organizes. For example, a non-profit organization makes events, sells a cause, and organizes its activities. A government makes services, sells them to its citizens, and organizes those activities as effectively as possible. Figure 11 provides an example of these functions.

THE COMPOSITION OF AN ORGANIZATION

MAKE	SELL	ORGANIZE
This is what an organization offers as a product or service.	This is what an organization does to sell what it makes.	This is what is organized in order to make and sell.
Production	Marketing	Technology
Operations	Sales	Strategy
R&D	Business Development	Finance
		Human Resources
		Procurement

Table 1. The composition of an organization breakdown

THE COMPOSITION OF AN ORGANIZATION

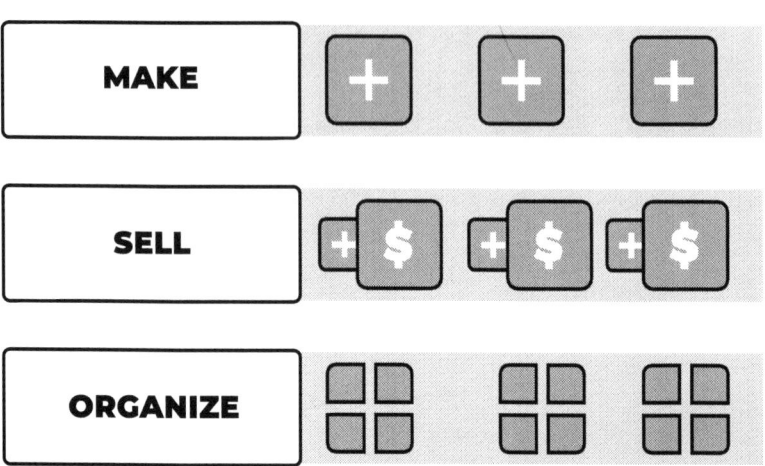

Figure 11. Visualization of the composition of an organization

Every growth hacker should take these three universal activities into account and work out which of the subsequent functions is the priority. For example, suppose a technology company wants to organize a way to sell its product more easily to those customers who prefer a flexible payment plan. To do this, it builds a payment plan that speeds up delivery and offers more than one way to pay.

The main idea for this hack is the technology used to build the payment plan. However, the technology feeds into marketing and leads to changes in operations (how the product is delivered). A growth hacker working on this project could identify these areas in order of priority to enhance the opportunities for hyper-growth.

The matrix in Figure 12 shows how growth hacking can work across different discipline.

The Cross-Functional Matrix

The cross-functional method brings into play three elements — first, a lead function, which in many cases may be technology; second, a support function, for example, marketing; and, third, a supplement function like operations.

The functions are broken down into the three core disciplines of an organization: Making, Selling, and Organizing. Making includes production and operations-related functions. Selling includes marketing, sales and business development functions. Organizing includes administrative and management functions design to steer, govern, and direct the organization, including the management of resources. This matrix enables you to see your organization's functional layout in one snapshot. From there, you can design your cross-functional growth hacks by determining your lead, supporting, and supplementary functions in priority sequence.

Cross functional growth hacking matrix

	Lead Function	Make			Sell			Organize				
		Production	Operations	R&D	Marketing	Sales	Bus. Dev.	Technology	Strategy	Finance	HR	Purchasing
Make Production												
Operations												
R&D												
Sell Marketing												
Sales												
Bus. Dev.												
Organize Technology												
Strategy												
Finance												
HR												
Purchasing												

Figure 12. Cross-functional growth hacking matrix

Now look at the matrix in Figure 13, with the lead function (technology) marked, and the subsidiary functions of marketing and operations numbered according to priority.

Technology + marketing + operations

Cross functional growth hacking matrix

	Lead Function	Make			Sell			Organize				
		Production	Operations	R&D	Marketing	Sales	Bus. Dev.	Technology	Strategy	Finance	HR	Purchasing
Make Production												
Operations												
R&D												
Sell Marketing												
Sales												
Bus. Dev.												
Organize Technology		X		3	2							
Strategy												
Finance												
HR												
Purchasing												

Figure 13. Example of how the cross functional growth hacks work

Ensuring that growth hacking works effectively for the functions you bring together is key to its success. By making growth hacking cross-functional, the opportunities for hyper-growth are even more likely.

Analytics

We've seen how experimentation and cross-functionality are key to making growth hacking effective. A successful growth hacker must be highly resourceful and creative. But, as we've seen, your growth hacking experiments will also need to be measurable. You will need to make use of analytics.

Analytics is what keeps the "true north" of a growth hacker focused on return of investment. They will help you find unforeseen ways to achieve growth. Opportunities you may have not thought about might lead to outstanding growth opportunities. However, without analyzing the results of your growth hack experiments, you'll never discover them. Analytics might even show you micro data within an exciting growth pattern that can greatly amplify your overall growth.

Analytics will also allow you to scale. If you know what's directly affecting your success, you can repeat it. From here, progressive learning can take place to amplify the repeatable components and lead to even better results. Without tracking, the right things, you can't repeat what has worked.

Finally, analytics can help you predict. No matter what insights you have, you will always be making a guess of what the future will look like. Understanding what you have in front of you, however, is your best predictor of growth. Creativity enables big possibilities others may not see; experimentation removes the mist from the mystery. By measuring what you test, you can make more accurate bets on the future.

We've seen how experimentation, cross-functionality, and analytics are the key components of a growth hacking mindset. Before discussing some of the practical tools you'll need, there's one more note to remember.

An anchoring characteristic of successful growth hacking is that the growth in question is focused primarily on the top line — i.e., revenue. Of course, profitability must be of concern because businesses that do not generate profits will fail. Traditionally, organizations seek growth through bottom-line efforts like cost cutting. Although these efforts do influence growth, however, they can only ever lead to *incremental* growth. They won't lead to the hyper-growth experienced by companies like Airbnb and PayPal. To experience hyper-growth, revenue must take priority over everything else—even costs.

Mindset of a Growth Hacker

Growth hackers consider every activity a company undertakes and thinks about to evaluate their impact on growth.

- If the activity has a **positive** impact, growth hackers amplify it.
- If it has a **negative** impact, they will try to find a way to create growth.
- If the activity has **no impact**, growth hackers will question whether there is an unknown secret they can unlock.

They use four forms of thinking to drive growth: drivers, reach, tooling, and decisions (Figure 14).

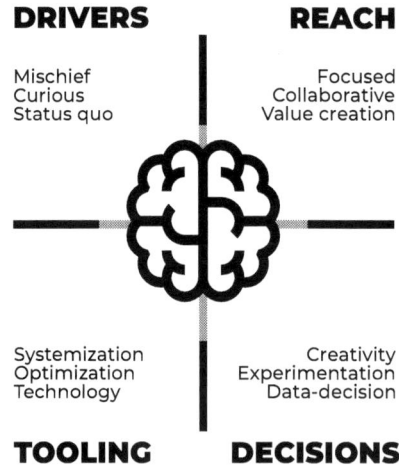

Figure 14. Growth hackers' mindset

These four primary areas represent what growth hackers think and how. This is how growth hackers focus all their efforts towards one direction and that direction is growth. Growth hackers are single-minded in nature and that is what makes them razor-sharp at what they do.

Top-Line vs. Bottom-Line Growth

By increasing sales, app downloads, and other cash-creating activity, growth hacking techniques focus on increasing the top line rather than the bottom line. In short, growth hacking prioritizes revenue as the driver of growth (Figures 15).

Growth hackers focus on top-line efforts to drive the gross revenue of an organization. Although profitability is important, if a growth hack is too costly with time, it will not be sustainable. Gross revenue driven activities are priority, but ensuring they are profitable is important.

Now that we've learned some mechanics behind how growth hacking works and discovered some of the key components and values, let's look at how growth hacking actually happens. To do this, we need to learn the tools of the trade.

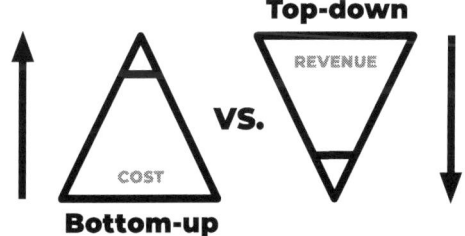

Figure 15. Top-line vs. bottom-up approach to growth

TOPLINE VS. BOTTOM-LINE APPROACH TO GROWTH AND GROWTH HACKING

	Top-line	Bottom-line
Strategy	Focused on developing new sources of revenue	Over-dependent on existing revenue streams
Gross revenue	The primary driver is fresh and new sources of revenue	The primary driver is cost cutting, then efficiency
Net revenue	Revenue is priority; costs are secondary	Costs are primary; revenue is secondary
Cost structure	Improved and adjusted; with time, gain more profitability	Adjusted immediately, but less profitable with time
Growth hacking	Primary approach; this is source of results with the most impact	Secondary approach; this supports primary growth activities and scaling
Summary	Top-line driven growth promotes innovation and disruption to build new revenue streams	Bottom-line growth focus on costs and efficiency which are important, but are not enough to grow

Table 2. Topline vs. bottom-line approach to growth

Technology and Traditional Businesses

Growth hacking isn't exclusively for technology companies. It can be applied across several traditional businesses and has been used for decades for corporate growth. A great traditional example is McDonalds, which in the 1950s–60s built their own billboards at freeway exits with high traffic to pull customers directly into their stores within 1–3 km of the freeway. This helped them growth hack during high traffic hours by targeting people when hungry on their way home.

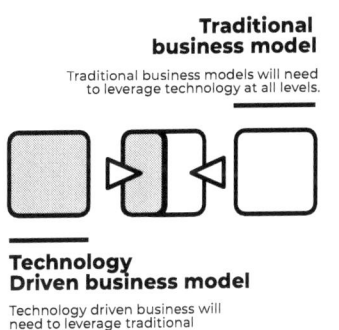

Traditional business model

Traditional business models will need to leverage technology at all levels.

Technology Driven business model

Technology driven business will need to leverage traditional business models.

technology

model

Blended business model

Technology and traditional business models can draw on growth hacking. However, there will always be a technology element that enables growth.

Figure 16. Technology vs. traditional business models and how they blend

Even if you're in a traditional business, technology will play a fundamental role in your success. This doesn't mean transforming your traditional business into a technology company, but instead leveraging technology to drive your growth. Technology offers a unique opportunity to acquire, retain, and grow customers at low costs and reach a wider range of customers who have an interest in your offering but whom you would not have not been able to reach and influence before.

Figure 16 illustrates how technology-driven models and traditional-driven models can work together. Where you will see technology stand out is in optimizing your operations, marketing, sales, and administrative functions to create more value. Even if you are running a Mom and Pop flower shop, you will be able to leverage technology to obtain and retain customers and expand your growth.

Types of Tools

It would be easy to simply provide a list of growth hacking tools here. However, unless you understand which of these tools you need to build the kind of growth you want, such a list wouldn't do you much good. In other words, what you want to achieve dictates which tools you're going to need. Full lists of tools are available in Bonus Chapter C, broken down by category.

Although there are a considerable number of useful tools available, not all of them are suitable for your startup. You must be discerning when selecting the best ones for your brand.

This book is above all a practical one, so I've provided a growth hacker's toolkit in *Bonus Chapter C: 88 Tools to Get You Started*.

The tools you can select fall into the following categories:

1. Task Automation
2. Analytics
3. Landing Pages
4. Feedback
5. Social Media
6. Marketing Automation
7. SEO (Search Engine Optimization)
8. PPC (Pay Per Click)
9. CRM (Customer Relationship Management)
10. Email Marketing Automation
11. Video and Image Creation

Before you select which of these to use, let's break down the different types of tools by their purpose.

The Benefits of Task Automation

Automation is one of the most powerful elements of successful growth hacking. To focus on growth, you need to streamline your operations. Spending hours on repetitive, detailed work will only slow your momentum. Using programs that can automate tasks for you, including user organization and management, is vital to your overall success.

Time spent working on the minute details of your business is time wasted. Instead, let automation tools handle much of the work for you. Here are three benefits you can expect from automation tools:

- Save Time. Focus on engagement and retention of new users.
- Save Money. Cut down on labor costs with less work.
- Fewer Errors. When machines handle the details, you don't have to worry about mistakes or falling behind.

Task automation leads both to scale and to optimizing growth hackers' ability to experiment, discover new hacks, and eventually implement new growth hacks,

The Benefits of Analytics

We talked about the importance of analytics earlier in this section. We also talked about experimentation and, as we've learned, you can't have one without the other. To focus your time and energy on tactics that are achieving growth, you need to discard anything that isn't generating the results you want. Without analytical tools, you could be wasting your resources on methods that aren't helping your brand.

Having the right information at your fingertips is crucial to maximizing your growth potential. Here are three reasons to include analytic tools in your workplace.

- Understand Your Customers. Know what users are responding to the most so that you can focus attention on those elements.
- Cut What Doesn't Work. Analysis enables you to remove any components that aren't generating a decent ROI.
- Streamline Your Operation. Put time and effort into programs that work so that your growth can be even faster.

Analytic tools are your decision-making magic wand that give you the ability to discover new possibilities, see what is and is not working, and why,

The Benefits of Landing Pages

Part of your growth hacking technique should be building a functional sales funnel that brings in new customers and converts them into sales. One of the easiest and most effective ways to do that is with high-quality, targeted landing pages. Landing pages are like an optimized store front with the purpose of conversion (sales).

Landing pages work because they encourage users to take action — whether that's signing up for a free product or subscribing to a mailing list. Building these pages and implementing them is essential to your success, so you'll need the appropriate software to help you.

Landing pages are integral to your marketing strategy because they can encourage users to take action (e.g., sign up for your product or subscriber list). Here are three reasons you want to automate this process with tools.

- A/B Testing. See which landing pages are the most effective by testing each one.
- Analyze Bounce Rates. Find out how frequently people are bouncing off of your pages so that you can fix the problem. (Bounce rates measure when users enter a page, but do not stay and, therefore, bounce out of the page.)
- Build Subscriber Lists. Killer landing pages can boost your growth hacking potential.

Landing pages enable you to draw in the traffic, engage potential customers, and monetize them.

The Benefits of Feedback

When you look at the success stories of companies that have utilized growth hacking to its full effect (Facebook, Uber, Airbnb, Hotmail), you'll notice one common reason for their success. All of these companies understood their user base to a remarkably accurate degree. By being laser-focused on your target audience, you're more likely to appeal to them and convert them into customers, even if your product is still in the development phase.

Businesses don't exist in a vacuum. You need to know what your customers are thinking and how they like what you offer. Here's why you want automated feedback tools to get information from your audience.

1. Increase Engagement. When users are asked about their opinions, they feel more connected to the brand.
2. Eliminate Redundancies. There may be parts of your product that people don't like. Getting feedback allows you to streamline and remove any unnecessary elements.
3. Understand Customers. Find out what components your audience values the most so you can cater to them.

Feedback is what keeps your grounded and alert to know what is and is not working. More importantly, feedback helps you discover new possible growth hacks.

The Benefits of Social Media

Growth hacking is about real growth, not vanity metrics such as likes, follows, and subscriptions. Although social media can be a tricky way to hack your way to growth, it's still an excellent platform to build buzz and get more people to see what you're about. Your audience is already on social media, so you should be too. Used carefully, social media is a viable part of the growth hacking process.

Automated tools can help you reach users on these platforms in the following ways.

- Increase Engagement. Most people want businesses to engage on social media. If you don't, then you're not as trustworthy.
- Increase Site Traffic. The more followers you get on social media, the more people you are likely to have visiting your site and your landing pages.
- Build Your Brand. Develop a brand identity and make more of an impact by rolling it out on various social platforms.

Social media is your pipeline of visibility to target, engage, attract, and monetize customers. It helps you gain visibility through influence driving your brand or cause.

The Benefits of Marketing Automation

Growth hacking is about creating supercharged marketing campaigns. Marketing has several components you'll need to track. Performing this manually can be time-consuming and laborious, so make use of marketing automation tools to save time, money, and costly mistakes. Marketing automation tools can assist with the following tasks:

- Email management
- Customer data
- Drip marketing (a flow of marketing content sent to customers over a period of time)
- Customer Relationship Management (CRM)

As you can imagine, having the right tools to take on those marketing tasks that are mundane and laborious can provide some real benefits. Here are three of them.

- Follow Up With Customers. Don't let new leads fall through the cracks. Instead, set up a drip marketing campaign to turn cold leads into hot ones.
- Stay Consistent. All too often, companies will have too much marketing or not enough happening at any given time. By automating your campaign, you stay on top of your message.
- Maintain Momentum. When starting your business, you may have ample time to focus on marketing. Once you get more clients, however, that will change. Automation tools enable you to continue marketing even when your time is limited.

Marketing automation optimizes the marketing system be bringing all the marketing processes together in one place to make effective marketing decisions.

The Benefits of SEO (Search Engine Optimization)

Search engine optimization (SEO) is a valuable tactic because it will make sure you get in front of your customers before anyone else. However, many businesses don't know how to tap into SEO effectively. Simply by having the right tools, you can optimize your site so that it ranks well in searches.

Here are some ways that SEO tools can assist your business.

- Keyword optimization
- Backlinks
- Update contact information
- Build a network of connections around your site

It's important to choose tools that make it easier to boost your rankings in Search Engine Results Pages (SERPs) so that you can grow even faster. Here are a few ways that SEO tools can make your efforts more effective.

1. Improve Rankings in Local Searches. When people are looking for a business nearby, is your company coming up? If not, these tools can make sure that you are.
2. Analyze Your Rankings. Get the data you need to improve your SEO tactics and build a better ranking in the process.
3. Streamline Your Site. If people are bouncing away from your pages too quickly, you will lose out to the competition. SEO tools can help you figure out how to make your site more user-friendly so that visitors boost your rankings.

SEO helps you optimize your ability to be founded or discovered when someone is trying to solve a specific problem. This targeted visibility should lead to direct monetarization.

The Benefits of PPC (Pay Per Click)

Pay per click is a cost-effective way of advertising on other websites and search engines like Google, so it's an effective tool in the growth hacker's arsenal. As you pay the search engine only when someone clicks on your advertisements, it's a cheap way to see which advertising methods work. To manage this process and get the most out of testing different advertisements, you'll need to make use of some PPC tools.

PPC tools enable your business to get noticed more quickly by allowing you to do the following:

- Run multiple PPC campaigns.
- Promote ads on different platforms.

- Customize your ads.
- Use analytics to know which ads work the best.

Best of all, because you're only paying for each click (rather than each view), you have a much higher chance of building a good conversion rate.

Once you start utilizing PPC marketing, you'll understand why it's such a powerful tool in the growth hacker's arsenal. Here are three top benefits of these tools.

- Improve Conversion Rates. When more people click on a landing page or CTA (click-to-action), the higher your chances are of converting leads to customers.
- Analyze Results. If your ads are not getting clicked on enough, perhaps you need to change your message.
- Customize Your Marketing. Once you test a few varieties to see which ads stick the best, you can improve your growth substantially.

PPC focuses on getting directly to customers who are searching for your solution, but don't know you exist or need to be reminded of your existence.

The Benefits of CRM (Customer Relationship Management)

Handling all those new customers who want to buy your product is a job in itself, and it's easy to let efforts slip at this stage. Delivering the best customer service is key to repeat customers and word-of-mouth recommendation, Use CRM tools to help with this process.

Customer relationship management is a system for keeping track of all of your customers throughout the sales process. Subscriber lists, email-marketing, follow-up campaigns —

all of these are handled with designated CRM tools. Some of these tools include:

- Email Management for organizing your emails into different lists for marketing purposes
- Correspondence so that you can create messages that are sent to customers automatically across various platforms
- Analysis that tracks data from customers and your relationship with them

These tools provide the following benefits:

- Operational Efficiency. Handle your correspondence with customers and interact with them.
- Thoughtful Analysis. See how your customers reacting to your outreach.
- Interdepartmental Collaboration. Help different departments work together to manage client relations.

CRMs provide ways to maximize your sales, marketing, and customer service efforts, and can provide behavioral data that can unravel new consumption patterns.

The Benefits of Email Marketing Automation

Automating how you communicate with potential customers will enable you to create a sales funnel (the sales process from customer awareness to revenue) and keep up with all your leads. You need several touch points with someone interested in your business to convert them into paying customers. Losing touch with this group of people will cost you clients.

Email marketing tools allow you to automate how you contact these potential customers. They help you follow up with emails a certain amount of time after the last contact. In this way, you can always be sure you're chasing those potential sales.

- Consistent communication. Contact your potential customers at regular intervals with the same message.
- Lead testing. See which leads are the most responsive to your marketing efforts.
- Multiple touch points. Ensure that potential clients stay interested with different types of marketing

Email automation optimizes your communications by lowering costs, keeping targeted, and maintaining and growing interest levels that eventually lead to direct monetization.

The Benefits of Video and Image Creation

Making sure your marketing and customer communication looks good will give you credibility in your industry. However compelling your communication is, if it doesn't have eye-catching images and videos, your customers may switch off.

Image- and video-creation tools can help you to create visuals for your marketing without breaking the bank.

- Creating Credibility. Make sure your communications look the part as well as sound good.
- Communication Variety. Offer your customers different types of content.
- Competitor Differentiation. Stand out from others in your field with eye-catching visuals.

Without creative communications, it will be hard to break through the noise. Therefore, optimizing new and advanced image and video technologies will help you attract new customers and retain existing ones.

Do You Need All These Tools?

Already we can see that there are a lot of tools you *could* use when running growth hacking experiments. But do you really need them all?

One of the reasons there are so many growth hacking tools is that many of them are designed for a single purpose — one tool promotes tweets, another sends follow-up emails to clients, and so forth. In addition, many new tools are launched daily and there are always major updates to existing tools. This variety makes shifting through them complex.

You need to focus on the tools that address your specific growth challenges and are usable, affordable, and scalable.

While this kind of focused attention can be useful, it doesn't help if you have to manage a dozen different programs as a result. If you can streamline your tools to just a handful while still being able to meet your goals, you'll be in much better shape. Not only do you have less work to do, but also it will be easier for your team to manage profiles and accounts. So choose your tools wisely, and select those that can perform more than one task where you can (Figure 17). Getting the right tools is about four steps. First is becoming aware of all the tools available. Second is selecting those who may potentially work. Third is evaluating the ones selected more carefully? Fourth is committing to the best of the key tools and using that tool.

GETTING YOUR TOOLS RIGHT
USING A BREAKDOWN EVALUATION METHOD OF
TOOLS HELPS ZERO IN ON THE BEST TOOLS

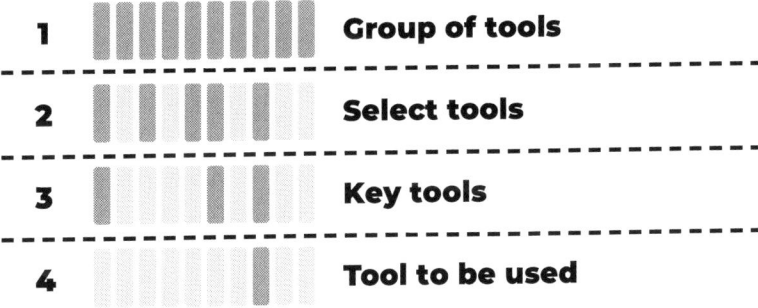

Figure 17. Getting the right tools in place for growth hacking

Work Smarter and Get Results

So how do you know which tools to use for your startup? The trick is to have a clear, defined objective for growth hacking from the start. While "growth" is the primary goal, if you break this down into more actionable steps such as getting more subscribers, achieving more downloads, increasing sales, etc., you'll have a more targeted purpose for your activities.

Once you've defined your purpose, it's easier to find the tools that will help facilitate that objective. If a tool isn't designed for that purpose, you don't need it — no matter how helpful you think it may be.

Getting Your Tools Right

There are three layers of tools you need to consider. The first are core tools that can work across many areas. They ideally have an ability to integrate across many other tools.

Core tools should provide a dashboard (a snapshot that summarize all vital data points) and analytics that give you a high-level view. You should be able to see how the tools themselves are performing. One of the primary roles of core tools is helping you determine:

1. Which channels are working best?
2. Which campaigns are best performing?
3. Which strategies overall got results?
4. Why have certain things worked and others not wor-ked?
5. What are the next steps to take?

The second layer — supporting tools — are ones that give your core tools the ability to go deeper. They have a performance-based aspect, but also a reach that your core tools do not have. They are function- or channel-specific, enabling your experiments, scaling, and the implementation of growth hacks. Such tools include landing page makers like Instapage (https://instapage.com/) or marketing automation tools like autopilot (https://www.autopilothq.com/)

The third layer — extension tools — give you more control and ability to go even deeper using support tools. These tools are used primarily for fine tuning, adjusting your offerings and other mechanisms to specific customers or changing needs. Such tools include plug-ins or add-ons that give more control.

You will need to develop a portfolio of tools across all three levels (Figure 18). With time, you will determine which combinations work best; eventually, as you grow, you will develop your own tools. By learning what has worked well and, especially, which tools have fallen short, you will discover where your own new tools will arise.

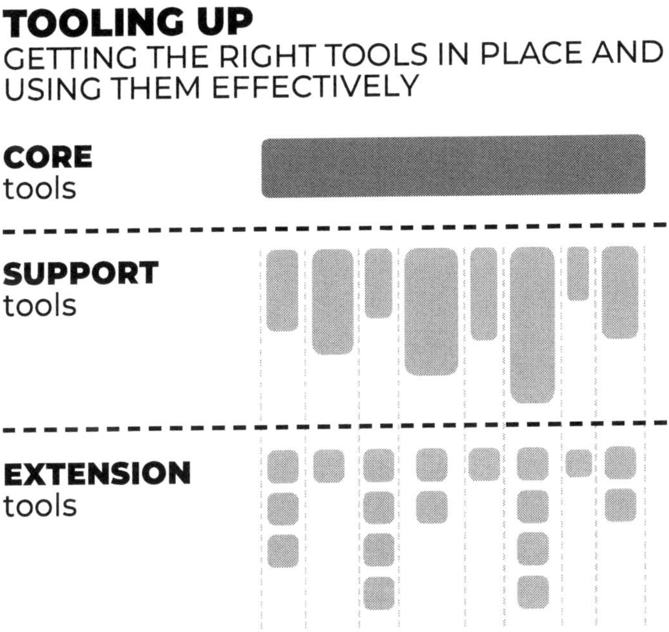
TOOLING UP
GETTING THE RIGHT TOOLS IN PLACE AND USING THEM EFFECTIVELY
CORE tools
SUPPORT tools
EXTENSION tools

Figure 18. Aligning and optimizing your tools

Understanding Your Tools

We've already identified a number of excellent growth hacking tools. You'll also find a comprehensive list in *Bonus Chapter C: 88 Tools to Get You Started* at the end of the book. Still, there are so many more tools out there, there's no way we could cover them all. As we've discovered, choosing your tools carefully is the key to success.

Once you've chosen which tools will work for you, the next step is to ensure you understand how they work. You'll need to practice and refine how you use each tool, just as you perfect everything else. Your goal is to focus your attention on the tactics that work rather than wasting time on ones that don't. If a tool in your toolkit isn't giving you a good return on investment, stop using it and replace it with something else.

Here are various ways to understand and refine the tools you are using:

Break Down Your Processes

Before you start downloading or buying software, make sure you know how you plan to use each program. Outline the different processes you regularly perform and then find the right tools to complete them.

Go into as much detail as possible so you can find out which tools will have the most impact. Ideally, each tool should help you streamline your operations (e.g., save time). Any tool that can help streamline should be on your short list.

Bundle Tools if Possible

Why work with a dozen different programs if you can accomplish the same goals with half a dozen instead? Again, your primary focus is to save time. Consolidate software that can be used for more than one purpose.

Test Each Tool Before Implementation

Just because a program sounds good on paper doesn't mean it will work for you when you start growth hacking. Test each tool to see how well it fits in with your operations; see if any improvements need to be made. Furthermore, see how well different programs work together. If they are incompatible, you may have to find a replacement solution.

5 Ways to Ensure Your Tools Are the Best

There are so many tools out there for growth hacking that it's hard to know which ones are ideal for your startup. Here are five ways to make sure that you're using the best ones for your particular needs.

1. *What Problem Is It Solving?* Don't use a tool just because it seems cool. Make a list of pain points and choose tools based on those.
2. *Can It Integrate with Other Tools?* Creating silos can interrupt your workflow. Try to find tools that can work together for a streamlined workflow.
3. *Is It Multifaceted?* Does the tool solve only one problem or can you use it for different aspects of your business? Try to consolidate into as few tools as possible.
4. *How Often Do I Use It?* Some tools may be useful only under specific circumstances. Make sure you're using your tools regularly, or eliminate them.
5. *Is It Cost Effective?* Don't pay for tools that aren't driving growth and building your business. They should be investments, not expenses.

How to Use Your Tools

One of the biggest problems startups face is that they have so many different methods at their disposal, they get overwhelmed. They spread themselves too thin and try to do too many things all at once. Avoid this problem by making sure you cultivate the right tools for growth. Before you start experimenting with growth hacks, it's a good idea to develop a plan to test and evaluate each of these tools.

Remember that you can always incorporate a new tool when you start a new growth hacking experiment. For now, focus on a few tools at once and then integrate more of them as you grow your business. Trying to do too much will leave you overwhelmed.

Here are some steps to follow when evaluating these your tools.

Step One: Align the tool with your growth challenge.

Understand your growth challenges well enough to determine which tools address your growth challenges directly and effectively. The better suited that a tool is for directly solving your growth challenges, the more effective that tool will be in helping you with your growth hacking strategies.

Step Two: Identify your objectives.

What is the specific goal for your growth hacking experiment? Perhaps you're trying to create content that will build up your authority online. Maybe you want to build a system for referrals. Whatever it is, make sure you understand your objective (e.g. writing and posting content).

Step Three: Identify what's stopping you from achieving your objective.

Suppose your current goal is to create and post content onto your blog, what's stopping you from doing that? Maybe you need an easy way to automate the posting process so you can be more consistent. Maybe you need to build the blog first.

Whatever is standing in your way, find the tool that will help you reach the next step. A good way to identify your obstacles is to break down your objective into specific items. Be as detailed as possible so you can figure out how a particular tool will help.

Step Four: *Identify what you need the tool to do.*

Once you've figured out the obstacles preventing you from executing your growth hack, think about what you need the tool to accomplish. Don't be tempted to look at the list of tools first, but determine what you need and go from there.

For example, if you need a tool to automate your posting schedule, think about the elements that tool should have. Will it need to share across social profiles, schedule days or weeks in advance, or post different types of content? Once you know what to look for, you can browse the list and see which tool fits best.

Step Five: *Consolidate the tools.*

Once you've identified some tools that could do the job, see if you could use any of them for other purposes. Look through the toolkit and take note of any option that seems like it could accomplish multiple objectives. Remember: you want to use as few tools as possible to reach the goal.

Step Six: *Evaluate ease of use.*

By now, you should have filtered our extensive toolkit to a handful that could accomplish your goal. The next step is to test each of these tools to see how easy it is to use. If there's a significant learning curve, remember that you won't be the only one using it. The tools you use should be simple and intuitive so that everyone on your team can use them.

Once you've figured out which tools are going to help facilitate your growth hacking ideas, put them in action! The only way to test how effective they are is to see how they perform in the real world. By choosing carefully, keeping it simple, and running frequent and effective tests, you'll identify the tools that will help your growth hacking succeed.

Your tools are you weapons. Today these tools have become highly accessible due to technology and lower entry price points. Additionally, many of today's tools are geared toward automation and integration, knowing that individual tools cannot operate alone anymore. Collectively, these tools give you a wide yet very powerful range of solutions to solve almost anything that will be needed to growth hack. Although there may be a limited number of tools that are directly related to your specific growth hacking today, many of the tools that exist directly lead into your overall ability to growth hack.

Summary

In this chapter, we have taken a deeper look into what growth hacking is, how growth hackers work, their approach, and tools used. We have covered the mind, model, and tools:

1. What growth hacking is, how growth hackers think, and how they function
2. Business models and the impact of technology on your business model for driving top-down vs. bottom-up growth
3. The types of tools that are needed and how to use them

When the mind, model, and tools are aligned, they are optimized in a creative manner towards growth. Growth hackers use all efforts toward one goal and that goal is growth.

CHAPTER NOTES

CHAPTER NOTES

Chapter 3.
Ready: to discover and unlock your strategy

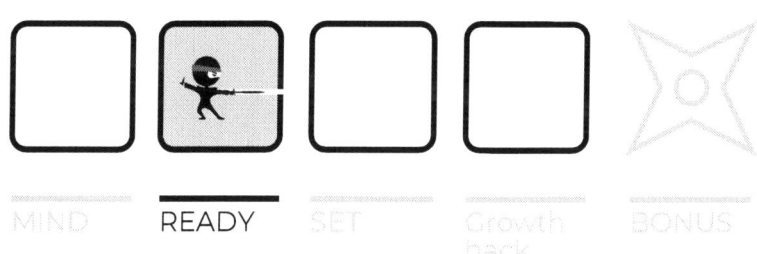

MIND   READY   SET   Growth hack   BONUS

In this chapter:

- Define what you *want to achieve* from growth hacking
- Understand your *product market fit* and how effective it is
- Discover what *makes your customers buy*

> **KEY TAKEAWAY:**
> *By discovering more about your business and your customers, you'll be in a stronger position to grow. Find profound insights that will lead to exponential growth.*

Now that you've learned the theory behind growth hacking and become familiar with your growth hacking toolkit, it's time to get READY to make growth hacking work for you. Every startup is different, so in this section we're going to discover how growth hacking can work in *your* industry and in *your* business. To do this, we're going to find out how to better understand:

- Your objectives,
- Your product,
- Your customers,
- And your team.

Understanding Your Objectives

It's not enough to know your product, define your customer, and understand your team. Before you build a growth hacking system, you also need to be clear about what you want to achieve. We talked about goals in the previous chapter, but now it's time to define your objectives and key results. We call these OKRs; they are made up of your goals and the measurable results you would expect to see when those goals are reached. By making your OKRs specific and measurable, you'll see if your methods are having the right impact.

Your objectives will be unique to your company, but below are some of the most common OKRs for growth hacking experiments. Note that each OKR has a set of measurable results that define its success:

Objective: to get more people to sign up for our email marketing campaign

- Key Result 1: to increase subscriptions by 25%
- Key Result 2: to increase user responses by 20%

Objective: to get more people to download and install our app

- Key Result 1: to achieve 100 downloads per week
- Key Result 2: to have 70% active users

Objective: to ensure that users are using the app regularly

- Key Result 1: to increase the number of active weekly users by 15%
- Key Result 2: to increase the number of active daily users by 20%

These objectives and key results can help inspire creative ideas and then develop these ideas into experiments. For example, a brainstorming session around the last OKR for a dieting app company might produce a number of ideas surrounding user retention. How can users be encouraged to continue using the app? Specific ideas might include introducing a reward scheme such as points for regular use, or making videos to go with the existing recipes. Once each experiment is implemented, analytics inform the company which methods have achieved the key results.

These are good examples of OKRs because they're specific, measurable, and focused on growth. Before you start running growth hacking experiments, try to come up with three-to-five objectives of your own, and several key results for each objective.

The most important aspect of your OKRs is that the key results are quantifiable and clearly defined. While an objective can be relatively generic (e.g., to increase sales), you need to know if and when you've met that objective. If your results are not quantifiable, then it will be impossible to tell if your experiment was successful.

You can (and should) change your OKRs as you move forward. Work not only on adjusting your results to build on your success, but come up with new objectives as well. For example, your initial OKRs may be geared towards increasing subscriptions. However, as your numbers grow, you might focus on user retention and satisfaction with the product.

Most importantly, remember that your framework is not rigid. If you come up with an objective that isn't worth the time or effort, or is too vague or difficult to achieve, don't be afraid to replace it. Be as versatile as you can and be honest about what you can achieve.

Understanding your product, your customers, and your team is the first step in getting ready to growth hack. Now it's time to start setting up your first experiments.

What Is Your Current Pain Point?

To find out how growth hacking can work for you, you need to work out the problem you're trying to solve. What's the biggest pain point for you at the moment (Figure 19)? Is your day spent organizing lists and managing emails? If so, you need to automate some of your tasks. If you find

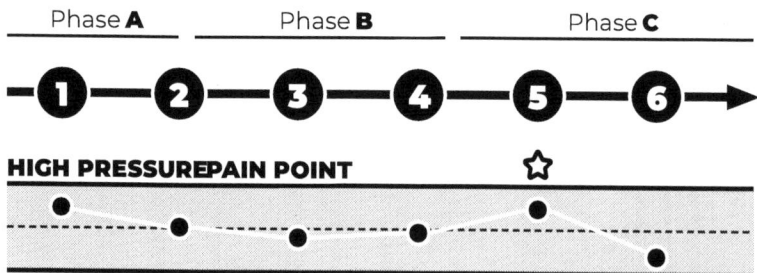

CUSTOMER JOURNEY MAP

Phase **A**   Phase **B**   Phase **C**

①—②—③—④—⑤—⑥→

HIGH PRESSURE PAIN POINT ☆

LOW PRESSURE PAIN POINT

☆ When analyzing the customer journey, it's vital to identify the **Pain Point** to know where to focus. The higher the Pain Point pressure is the bigger **opportunity** there is to **solve a problem** that will add significant **value**

Figure 19. Customer experience journey mapping and finding customer pain points

yourself struggling to keep up with consistent social media posting, then you'll need an app or program that can do it for you. Better still, if you can combine these two applications to work together you could maximize your efficiency even more.

What Is Your Primary Growth Goal?

Next, you need to be specific about what you want to achieve. What's your main objective for growth? To increase pre-sales? To build downloads? What's going to help your startup make money quickly? If you're selling a physical product you'll face different challenges than if you're selling services or digital products.

When we look at the most successful growth hacking examples, there's one thing they have in common. They exist (mostly) in the digital world. Companies like Dropbox, Facebook, and AirBnB aren't selling physical products, but digital ones.

If you're starting a company where you need infrastructure and manufacturing, you'll have different growth goals than a digital company. Getting people to download an app is one thing, but getting them to buy a physical product is something else.

Begin by understanding your goals and objectives to ensure you have clarity and focus (Figure 20). Without clarify and focus, the rest of your efforts will not align effectively. Developing this understanding is an important part of getting on your way to hyper-growth.

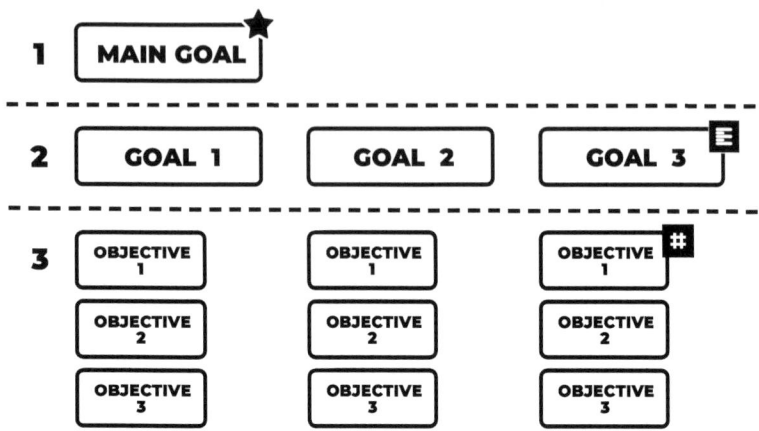

Figure 20. Goal and objective hierarchy and structure

Understanding Your Product

Having a viable and scalable product is at the heart of successful growth hacking. It does not matter how well you implement a growth hack strategy. Without a product people want to buy, scalability won't make any difference at all. In other words, if the demand for a product isn't viable, the product will not experience success, even if it's scalable. You can always develop scalablity once a product has proven its demand. Scalablity has its own complications and investment.

We're going to take a minute to dive into your product and ensure you have the best possible foundation for your growth hacking strategies. If your product needs tweaking, now is the time to do it. To understand more about your product and why people will want it, try asking the following questions.

- Do you have a viable product?
- Do people want your product?

- What need does it serve?
- How easy is it to pitch?
- What's your competition?
- Is your product scalable?

Do You Have a Viable Product?

While you don't necessarily have to have a tangible product ready to go before promoting it and growing your brand, you need to be on the right track to deliver it to your customers sooner rather than later. Part of the startup process can be getting people to sign up during the development phase as a means of building capital. Unless you know that you can deliver on that promise, however, you should not market it yet.

Suppose you have an idea for a world-changing app, but you haven't started building code for it yet. First talk to some programmers to see what it will take to develop the app before pitching the idea to investors or consumers.

Product Research

You won't be able to hack your way to growth if you have a product that no one wants. First make sure that your product is as viable as possible. Here are five ways to do that.

1. Talk to Customers. Find out what they value, what they're looking for the most, and how they want the product delivered.
2. A/B Testing. Try out multiple functions and elements of your product to see which ones receive the best responses.
3. Get Crowdfunding. Ask consumers to invest in your product, even if it's a demo. If they're willing to put money down, you have a viable product.

4. Build a Subscriber List. Use landing pages to build a list of leads and potential customers.
5. Look at the Competition. See what other companies are doing. Pay attention to what works and why.

Do People Want Your Product?

You can have the tools in place and a world-class growth team on your payroll, but if no one wants your product, none of it will matter. Even the best marketing tactics won't work if the item itself is unnecessary, badly designed, or poorly produced.

A great way to validate your product or idea is to talk with people about it. See what their reaction is. If they're clamoring for it from the beginning, you know that you're poised for growth. If the response is tepid, then you need to review your development before thinking about any potential hacks.

Product Viability

Product viability means that there is enough of a market for your business not only to succeed initially, but also to grow. Part of testing that viability is making sure your product is desirable in the first place. Here are five ways to test for that.

1. Create a Solution. Figure out a problem that customers are having and find a solution that meets their needs.
2. Test Sell Your Product. Even if you're still in development, sell the product as if it exists and see what the response is.
3. Build Buzz. Advertise your release and see whether people are eagerly anticipating what you have to offer.
4. Get Feedback. Ask customers what they like and dislike about your product.

5. Incentivize Referrals. If people love your product, they will share it and talk about it. Create a referral program and see how well it does.

What Need Does It Serve?

Although not all products are used for practical purposes, there should be a compelling reason for people to buy it. Whether it solves a particular pain point or offers a level of satisfaction that's not easily attained, your customers should be eager to buy what you're selling.

Airbnb provides an excellent example. There was a decline in tourism spending for hotels because tourists wanted better experiences for less. Airbnb recognized the need for an outstanding experience for an affordable price, creating value. Their first growth hack in addressing this need was in their business model — not building or acquiring real estate, but rather renting it on demand. Second, part of their growth hack was to create revenue opportunity that would increase the need for value creation by properly owners. These two hacks combined gave the momentum to fulfill a need that was not being served.

Another more traditional example is FedEx. They recognized the need for reliable yet affordable overnight delivery. Their growth hack was about a promise using their disruption systems to ensure packages would arrive first thing the next morning, insured in case something goes wrong, and for an affordable price.

How Easy Is It to Pitch?

Although the product itself is the backbone of your business, you also have to be able to sell it quickly and easily. If you're spending a lot of time explaining what your product is and why people should care, you'll lose out to the competition.

When designing a pitch, be as concise as possible. How would you describe your product in a single sentence? What about in three words? As you develop your sales pitch, test it out on a variety of people to see what the response is and adjust it accordingly.

A great example of this is Uber, where all you have to do is say where you are and where you want to go. Only two important inputs and you're on your way. Uber has not exposed any of the backend friction points within the process to the customer and burdening them with it. Their easy pitch is *instant mobility*.

Another more traditional example is McDonalds, which introduced new kiosks to replace waiting times at the casher. They simple cut out the wait time by simplifying the process of just selecting what you want, paying, and getting your food. Their easy pitch is *walk-in convenience***.**

What's Your Competition?

No matter how innovative your product is, the chances are someone else is either already making it or they offer something similar. What's your competition and how can you differentiate your product so it stands out? Perhaps you're making a service easier for users or improving on a current product. If so, highlight these improvements when pitching your product.

Identifying your competitors and what they're doing will give you a clearer idea of how to stand apart from them. Even in a crowded market, the right hook can make all the difference, provided you have the right product to back it up.

Is Your Product Scalable?

Part of the reason that digital companies like Facebook can proliferate is that they don't need lots of infrastructure to scale. Servers and storage space are relatively easy to come by, especially when compared to a storefront selling physical products. When you develop your growth strategy, ask yourself how quickly you can scale up production to meet demand. Assess the roadblocks that might prevent you from doing so; then find people who can help you overcome those obstacles.

Product Scalability

Since growth hacking is all about building your business as quickly as possible, you need to make sure that there is room to grow. Here are five points to consider before pulling the trigger.

- What's the Demand? If people aren't clamoring to get their hands on your product, growth may be a lot slower than you like.
- What's the Competition? How many other businesses offer what you have? Can they provide it faster and better than you?
- What's the Buzz? Are leads coming in regularly or in spurts? When testing new landing pages, are you getting more leads or less?
- What's the Churn Rate? How many new users are dropping your product shortly after buying it? Can you fix that?
- What is Your Cost of Acquisition? If it costs more to get new customers than the money you're bringing in, you're destined to fizzle out and fail sooner rather than later.

As we've seen, the most famous growth hacks so far have had one thing in common: they existed in a digital format. Try to imagine Uber getting so big so fast if the company had to buy and maintain a fleet of vehicles. Imagine Airbnb taking on the hotel industry if it had to do site inspections for each location and get permits for all of its properties.

It's easy to scale up when all you have to do is build an app or increase your server space to meet demand. It's much harder to grow exponentially when you have to invest in infrastructure or product development along the way.

If you do have a physical product, these challenges shouldn't deter you from focusing on growth hacking. If you can create demand, it will be easier to find a way to get the supply. Once people see how desirable your product is, you'll be more likely to find investors to back your idea.

Whatever your product, have a plan in place for scaling. To do this, consider the best-case scenario. What if you had to produce 100,000 units in six months? How would you do that? If your product is digital, you'll have a much smoother transition from small startup to successful business, but you should still have a plan in place to ensure your company doesn't collapse under its own weight.

Understanding Your Customers

Understanding your customers goes hand in hand with understanding your product. You should be researching your customers while developing your product. Unless people are buying what you're selling, it won't matter what you create.

Whether you're growth hacking a startup or an established business, creating a buyer persona can go a long way toward ensuring success. Try to get into the minds of your ideal user by keeping the following elements in mind.

Be Focused, Not Broad

One of the most common reasons that marketing campaigns fail is they target too many people. It may be appealing to market your brand to as many leads as possible. However, when you consider that each lead has different needs, it's impossible to connect with each one when you're using a generic approach.

The best way to build an audience quickly and to get the most out of your growth hacking techniques is to focus your attention on a particular set of customers. For example, rather than trying to appeal to all teenagers, develop a campaign for teenage males between 13–16 who are interested in football, or target teen girls between 14–18 who love arts and crafts.

When creating buyer personas, remember: the more detailed you can get, the more successful you will be. Find out exactly how your product will satisfy a need for your customer. By focusing on one type of person, it will be easier to figure out what that person wants and create a buzz around your product.

Start Niche, Build Organically

One of the ways to ensure you can focus on a specific group of customers is by starting with a niche product. Instead of trying to reach millions of people, concentrate on getting a handful of people interested. Large-scale growth may be your ultimate goal, but to get there, sometimes you need to start small. Ten users can turn into 20, and 20 can turn into 40; starting niche doesn't prevent you from gaining new customers as your company grows.

Another thing to remember is that you can focus on more than one buyer persona at a time. Just because you've developed one buyer persona doesn't mean that you can't market to another as well. If you think that more than one type of person will appreciate what you're selling, create different personas for those two groups. Then you can build a marketing campaign for each persona so that you can connect with your audience that much faster. Remember: these two groups might have clear distinctions, so don't give them the same message. Appeal to them in unique ways and you'll see better results.

Learn the Adoption Curve

When creating different marketing tactics, it helps to know and understand the customer adoption curve. Figure 21 shows a simple bell curve that illustrates how well your product will be received over time.

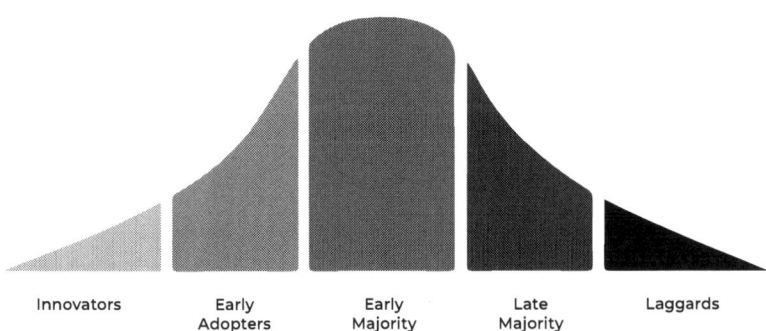

Figure 21. Technology/innovation adoption curve

At the front of the curve are the innovators. These are the people who are always looking for the next big thing. Innovators are crucial during the development phase because their feedback can help you make improvements to both your product and your marketing tactics.

After the innovators come the early adopters. They are not as forward-facing as innovators, but they like to be first in line for new products, especially the ones that seem chic or trendy. Again, you can use early adopters to your advantage to further refine your approach before it gets to the masses.

At the height of the curve is the early majority. This section is where you will see the most significant spike in your user base. If all goes well, the peak won't deflate too much as more and more people buy and use your product. A drop in users here means you still have work to do to adjust either your pitch or your product.

Finally, there is the late majority and the laggards. Typically speaking, these are the people who wait until a product or service has been around for a while before adopting it. These are the users who prefer taxis because it's what they know, but after riding in an Uber with a friend, they decide that it might be worth downloading the app.

Each of these groups of people presents different challenges for your company, so make sure you understand how they differ and how you can appeal to each one. For example, the perks that brought the innovators to your product probably won't be tempting for the late majority, so you'll have to come up with a different selling point for those users when the time comes.

5 Ways to Ensure You Know Your Customers Well

A large part of growth hacking is connecting and engaging with your audience. The better you know your customers, the easier it is to sell your product to them. Here are five ways to ensure that you get the right information about your user base.

- Ask Questions. During the sales process, ask customers about what they value the most.
- Conduct Surveys. Follow up with customers to find out how well the product is working for them.
- Create a User Profile. Rather than focusing on a group, create a profile based on a single individual.
- Encourage Reviews. Make sure that customers are posting reviews online and read what they have to say.
- Use Social Media. See what customers are saying about your business and product on social platforms.

Understanding Your Team

Just as different growth hacking tools will help you build your audience, your growth hacking team is integral to your brand's success. You'll need to understand the strengths and weaknesses of everyone on your team so that you can manage them as efficiently as possible.

Talk with each person individually to find out what they can do. Then think about how you could merge talents to achieve better success. If one person is great at coding and another is excellent at graphic design, they could work together to build compelling landing pages for your site and embed marketing materials across different mediums.

Also consider the ideal workload for each member of your team. Some people can work for hours straight whereas others may need regular breaks throughout the day to be as productive as possible. Everyone is different. Manage each person as an individual rather than forcing them all to adhere to the same rules. By accommodating different work methods, you'll achieve maximum productivity while also cultivating loyalty and teamwork.

5 Ways to Ensure that You Have the Best People

Having a high-quality growth hacking team is essential for long-term success. However, just because someone is qualified doesn't mean that he or she is the right fit for your company. Here are five ways to ensure you have the right team.

- Do They Work Well Together? Everyone should be collaborating and working together to drive growth. Team members who work individually can disrupt a smooth workflow.
- Do They Want the Same Goal? You want to avoid having people who view your startup as "just a job." Make sure that your team is enthusiastic about where your business is headed.
- Are They On the Same Page? Having a clear mission statement can help. However, if team members are focusing on different priorities, it can lead to disruption.
- Are They Getting Results? Although growth hacking isn't an exact science, you can tell if someone is delivering results or not. If not, it's time to make cuts.
- Are They Satisfied? Workers who don't like the job are going to sink your company faster than anything else. Make sure everyone is happy with the way things are going. If not, find out why and make changes if necessary.

Regardless of how small or large your team is, everyone needs to be on the same page when testing and implementing growth hacking strategies. Here are some crucial elements to consider when bringing everyone up to speed.

Inspiration

One of the most important things to create in your team is inspiration. Growth hacking is essentially a creative process, so you'll need a team that can brainstorm and bounce ideas around.

Inspiration creates experimentation. In turn, experimentation is crucial to growth hacking. First, experimentation allows you to capitalize on your successes and learn from your failures so that you can continue to build knowledge and create momentum.

Second, it allows you to come up with unique strategies that will ensure your growth continues. Lack of inspiration within the team is one of the main reasons growth hacking fails.

If you continue to do the same thing, you'll get the same results. In time your growth hacking experiments will fizzle out. Find inspiration wherever you can so you and your team can keep coming up with new ideas for growth hacking experiments.

Finding Inspiration

Because inspiration is so valuable, you need a strategy for finding and leveraging it. Here are some tips.

- Look at the Competition. See what other successful companies are doing and analyze why their tactics work.
- Get Insight From Customers. What are they responding to the most and what do they want to see in the future?
- Look at Past Failures. Even your worst ideas can have nuggets of wisdom. Go back through them and see if there are any pieces you can repurpose for new growth hacks.

Communication

Communication between you and your team members is essential. A cohesive system that works fluidly relies on everyone communicating effectively. Whether you communicate through weekly meetings with all team members or you have a manager who can see everything from a broader perspective and discuss ideas with team members one to one, make sure you have a clear system of communication in place.

Achieving Communication

Preparing worksheets and learning from your previous mistakes may be easy for you. It's imperative, however, that your team understands each success or failure and why it worked (or didn't). Thus, you must establish strong communication standards within your team. Here are some ways to do that.

- Get Feedback. Ask team members why they think specific hacks failed or succeeded. Learn their takeaways from the experience.
- Ask for New Ideas. See what your team develops for new hacks.
- Share Results. Whether a hack passes or fails, be sure to update the group along the way.
- Encourage Collaboration. Make sure that different departments work together to achieve your goals. Encourage them to share ideas.

Documentation

Ideally, you'll retain your team members for the duration of your growth hacking campaign. However, that may not always be the case. Therefore, make sure everyone keep updated records of progress. If someone leaves the team without a detailed written and verbal handover, all of their knowledge goes as well.

Come up with a system for recording and sharing data. If necessary, make the data available to the whole team or at least make sure your team leader has full access.

Maintaining Documentation

Documenting your successes and failures is crucial if you're going to understand why something worked and make adjustments for your next hack. If you don't record progress with worksheets and data, it will be easy to fall into the same traps.

Overall, make a habit of recording everything that happens with your growth hacks. Create forms and an automated system for filling out and collecting them.

Then, be sure to read and analyze these documents regularly so that you can understand and interpret the information. Documentation is worthless unless you use it.

Transparency

Finally, make sure everything you do in your growth hacking experiments is accessible to everyone on the team. Transparency breeds trust and confidence among team members. It also is easier for everyone to understand where you are and where you're headed. Make numbers available to all; be sure to update the team on any progress. A team that sees the results of their hard work are more likely to feel inspired to build on that success.

Building Transparency

When your team sees what everyone else is doing; they are much more willing to share in the successes and failures of the company. Transparency ensures that everyone is held accountable for his or her actions; it also can inspire collaboration and open dialogue at all times. Here's how you can achieve better transparency.

Have staff sit in on management meetings. By including team members, supervisors will be more aware of what they are saying. Encourage feedback as well. Share data with everyone involved in the hack. When people see how well a tactic is doing, they will feel more connected to its success.

Encourage feedback. Make sure that all team members feel like they can address any issue at any time.

Summary

In this chapter, we have prepared by understanding four key factors related to your business before you can start to grow. We have looked at:

1. Your Objectives. Clarify your goals and objectives so that you are heading in the right direction.
2. Your Product. Your offering should be optimized with a good product market fit, ensuring there is demand.
3. Your Customers. Know who your customers are exactly in order to align objectives and product to customers.
4. Your Team. Prepare yourself internally and externally so your team is ready for growth.

Creating these master alignments ensures you're ready for growth. If you're not ready, it is important to get organized because this phase is vital moving forward. Without being ready, your subsequent efforts will face serious challenges.

CHAPTER NOTES

CHAPTER NOTES

Chapter 4.
Set: your experiments and development ideas

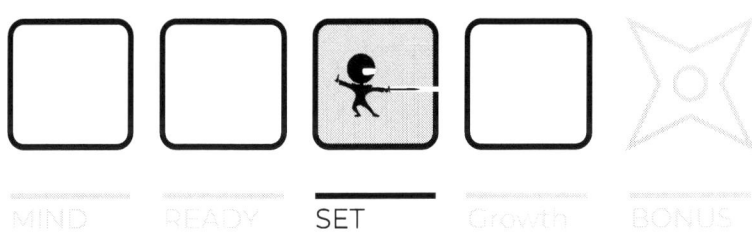

MIND   READY   **SET**   Growth   BONUS

In this chapter:

- Learn the *growth hacking cycle* and how to run successful experiments
- How to run small, quick, and cost-effective *experiments*
- Some Dos and Don'ts of *conducting growth hacking* experiments

> **KEY TAKEAWAY:**
> **To make your growth hacking strategy sustainable in the long term, you need to limit how much time, money, and effort you invest in each experiment.**

The heart of growth hacking is experimentation. Have you been in a situation where people's opinions, including your own, dominate your direction? Recognize that those opinions are untested and form your whole view, often blinding you from other possibilities and leading to less flexibility, responsiveness, insights, and eventually failure.

Experimentation is designed to mitigate failure by removing opinions and letting data tell us the truth. Beyond that, experimentation allows us to discover new possibilities we did not see before. Solid processes help create a growth system that allows experiments to find new and better ways to grow.

This chapter focuses on how to run well-structured experiments that lead to scalable and sustainable growth.

GROWTH SYSTEM
PROCESSES THAT ENABLE GROWTH

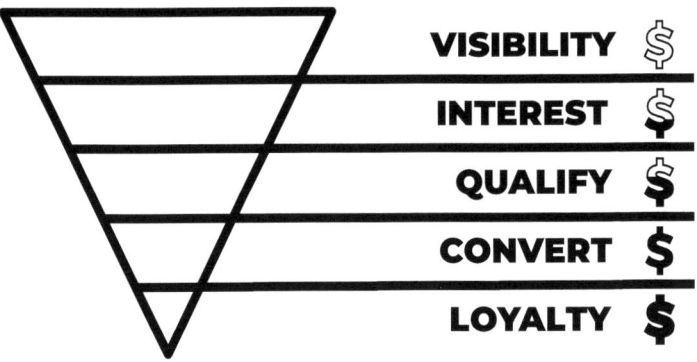

Figure 22. Growth system

Before experimenting and driving growth, it's vital to understand the fundamentals of creating a growth system (Figure 22). In essence, a growth system is a drill-down, filter-style process.

1. Visibility is getting your brand and offering in front of prospects that may have an interest in your offering.
2. Interest is transforming visibility into a desirable attitude towards your offering that engages potential customers.
3. Qualify transforms desire into potential sales by filtering potential customers among those who would want to buy now, later on, or may need some encouragement to buy.
4. Convert is the transformation of qualified customers into actual revenue.
5. Loyalty is about customer service support and recycling the growth process. It transforms existing customers into greater revenue or a channel where you can generate increased sales through their own network or endorsement of your offerings.

The growth system is a systematic drill-down process that is quickly, efficiently, and cost-effective in turning potential interest into revenue. What is important about a successful growth system is its ability to do two main things. First is having a high conversion rate and the ability to convert loyalty to more sales. The conversion rate is about keeping the customer acquisition cost low. Second is having the ability to convert more existing customers into more business, as these two factors are vital in profitable and scalable growth.

Master Experimentation

Experimentation is at the core of growth hacking; you need to master it. Experimentation allows the best ideas to rise and weaker ones to move out of the way. This level of focus and open-minded approach removes bias and helps data emerge to find growth. You'll need to make use of the tools and techniques available, but you'll also need to be smart about your experiments.

This chapter includes several sets of exercises (Figure 23):

1. Growth problem (Exercises 1–4)
2. Growth hacking experiments (Exercises 5–10)
3. Growth hacking extensions (Exercises 11–16)

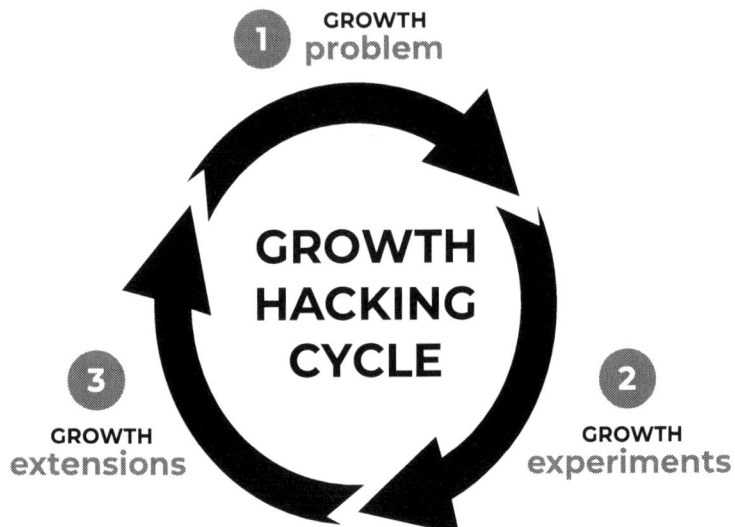

Figure 23. Growth hacking cycle

Growth Problem

Before being able to hack growth, you must understand what your growth problem actually is. This is critical because it's important to be specific and focused. Usually there is a large growth problem at play. However, without breaking the problem down and tackling smaller parts, you won't succeed in solving the larger growth problem itself.

READY FOR GROWTH			
Preparing by defining and managing the growth problem itself			
Growth Area	**Growth Challenge**	**Growth Issue**	**Growth Ideas**
In which area do you have a growth challenge?	*What is the specific growth challenge itself?*	*Describe how the sub-problem is preventing or slowing down growth.*	*Develop three initial growth hacking ideas to solve this growth problem.*
Select	Select	Describe	List
			1
			2
			3

Table 3. Ready for growth

Growth Area

Your growth problems stem from the following business functions within your organization. Several functions may be involved, but you need to find the root cause.

Competition	Financial	Product/Service
Technology	Strategy	Team
Recruitment	Marketing	Operation
Culture	Sales	R&D
Structure	Management	

EXERCISE 1: GROWTH AREA

Select one of the 13 functions listed above or, if not listed, create one: Select only one business function as your primary growth problem area. Although there may be a cascading effect, it's important to focus on the root cause.

Exercise 1. Growth Area

Select the area, which represents your primary growth problem. Then systematically tackle one growth problem at a time, even if it's a smaller part of the large growth problem.

Growth Challenge

In general there are seven high-level sorts of growth challenges. Not all growth challenges are limited to these seven, but they do cover most of the challenges. It's important to classify your growth challenge. This helps you tackle it better. It also aligns members of your team and others who may be working with you on the growth hacks themselves. These seven areas are:

1. Too much demand
2. Too little demand
3. No demand at all
4. Not enough resources, but can acquire
5. Not enough resources, but cannot acquire
6. Not enough resources, but can be fixed
7. Doesn't exist

EXERCISE 2: GROWTH CHALLENGE

Select one of the seven reasons why you're facing a growth challenge. Although you may have more than one reason, it is important to focus on the primary growth challenge.

Exercise 2. Growth Challenges

If your growth challenge doesn't exist, the resources needed may not exist. Instead you may have to work from scratch — not an impossible task — but it's important to know where you stand and how to tackle these challenges using growth hacking.

Growth Issue

Once you have defined the problem and challenge, you need to describe the growth issue in context. This is a high-level statement, roughly 2–3 sentences that summarizes the growth issue itself. The statement should be truthful, explicit, and comprehensive in describing what the real growth problem is. The clearer this statement is, the better your ability will be to solve the problem. At the end, you do not want to be solving the wrong problem. You need to be focused on the right growth issue.

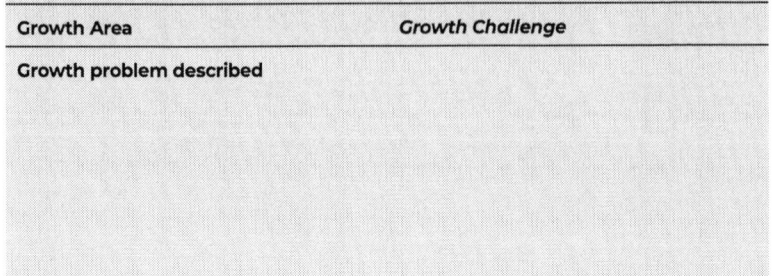

EXERCISE 3: GROWTH ISSUE

Remind yourself of the context, but writing down the growth area and challenge. Then describe the growth issue itself as a problem statement. Keep it simple, short, and very focused within the context of the growth problem itself.

Growth Area	***Growth Challenge***

Growth problem described

Exercise 3. Growth Issue

Growth Ideas

Identify three high-level ideas per growth problem you tackle. These ideas are rough, broad, and top-line style solutions to solve this growth problem. They are not meant to be detailed — those details will be defined and sorted out in growth hacking experiments.

EXERCISE 4: GROWTH IDEAS

Brainstorm three high-level ideas as a path to potential solutions for the specific growth issue you defined in Exercise 3: Growth Issue

Exercise 4. Growth ideas

Once you have generated your growth ideas, *carry them throughout the growth experiments* in the following exercises. Each idea should reflect a name that defines the experiment to be undertaken. You will be developing these ideas into experiments in the following exercises.

Growth Hacking Experiments

The growth hacking process itself is rooted in experimentations. Experiments are designed to resolve the growth problems defined in the previous section. Bring each growth idea forward and include their name in an experiment name that reflects the nature of the experiment itself. When you have three ideas or more testing per growth problem, it is important to prioritize which ones to resolve first. It's best to experiment one growth idea at a time rather than attempt all at once, at least in the beginning until you have more growth hacking experience.

FPL GROWTH HACKING EXPERIMENTS
Fail, Pass, Learning System

Experiment	OKR	Tools	Growth Hack	FPL	Outcome
Name the experiment.	*Define a single measure.*	*List all the tools for the experiment.*	*If yes / retesting pass, run the growth hack.*	*Fail, pass, or learn results from experiment.*	*List the next steps after the results*
Name — Describe	Measure	List	Name	Select	Select
				☐ PASS ☐ FAIL ☐ LEARNING	☐ YES — Ready to go; lets scale hack ☐ RETEST: for strength or adjustment ☐ NO - Discard

Table 4. FPL Growth hacking experiments

The FPL Fail, Pass, Learning system is core to the experimentations (Figure 24). The system helps you design, monitor, and record result. The FPL system is designed to capture learning from both pass and fail experiments, then transform them into new ideas that become growth hacks. This way you have a sustainable system of capturing, designing, and testing new growth hacks throughout the whole exercise.

Experiment

Take the growth hacking ideas generated to solve growth problems. Name it into an experiment reflective of its goal.

EXERCISE 5: GROWTH IDEA EXPANSION	
Bring your growth ideas from previous exercises. Expand them by generating another three ideas on how to develop that single high-level growth idea. You can generate many more than three but, for the sake of this exercise, we will focus on three expanded ideas per growth idea	
Growth Idea 1	**Expanded Ideas**
	1
	2
	3
Growth Idea 2	**Expanded ideas**
	4
	5
	6
Growth Idea 3	**Expanded Ideas**
	7
	8
	9

Exercise 5. Growth idea expansion

The next step is to take these expanded ideas and turn them into experiments. The experiments are designed to be simple, small, and cost effective. You should be able to complete them within a short timeframe. Focus on a single measure for the experiment.

EXERCISE 6: GROWTH EXPERIMENTS

Expanding on the previous exercise, take each expanded idea and design a simple, small, and cost-effective experiment to determine if it is a fail or pass.

Expanded Idea 1	Experiment
Expanded Idea 2	Experiment
Expanded Idea 3	Experiment
Expanded Idea 4	Experiment
Expanded Idea 5	Experiment
Expanded Idea 6	Experiment
Expanded Idea 7	Experiment
Expanded Idea 8	Experiment
Expanded Idea 9	Experiment

Exercise 6. Growth Experiments

OKR (Objectives and Key Results)

You will want to have single, specific achievement measures that define if an experiment passes or fails when testing. These measures need to be very objective in nature.

EXERCISE 7: OKR

For each experiment, create a single measure for testing. This measure should be something that can clearly determine a fail or pass without distortion or misrepresentation.

Experiment 1	OKR
Experiment 2	OKR
Experiment 3	OKR
Experiment 4	OKR
Experiment 5	OKR
Experiment 6	OKR
Experiment 7	OKR
Experiment 8	OKR
Experiment 9	OKR

Exercise 7. Objective and key results

Tools

Most experiments will require tools — whether third party or your own — to conduct the experiments themselves. List all the tools needed and their roles.

EXERCISE 8: TOOLS FOR EXPERIMENTS

For each experiment, you may need various tools that help you conduct the experiment. The best of these tools have the measurements and analytics in them to help you determine a fail or pass.

Experiment 1	Tools
Experiment 2	Tools
Experiment 3	Tools
Experiment 4	Tools
Experiment 5	Tools
Experiment 6	Tools
Experiment 7	Tools
Experiment 8	Tools
Experiment 9	Tools

Exercise 8. Tools for experiments

> **Let's Start Growth Hacking**
>
> *Once your experiment is designed and tools are selected, it is time to start growth hacking — putting it to action now.*

Growth Hack

The key moment has arrived; time to execute that growth hack. To give this step some life, give it a nice name that inspires you, drives interest, and clearly labels it.

EXERCISE 9: GROWTH HACK

Name and describe your growth hack here. Have some fun with the name and the description.

Name of Growth Hack

Description

Exercise 9. Growth hack

FPL System (Fail, Pass, Learn)

The fail, pass, learn system is a dynamic and objective approach that concludes all experiments and, with learning, enables more progressive hacks. Learning enables experiments to develop into a sustainable system, whereas pass or fail can be transformed into learning and then into ideas that feed new experiments (Figure 24).

This feed of new experiments allows growth hackers to focus by drawing on resources and capabilities already used, without letting them going to waste. This process provides a platform for growth hackers to see meta-patterns — for example, a series of experiments may be failing, but collectively have an extremely high learning value that can lead to significant growth.

Failures are constructive because they give clues about what not to do as well as changes that might reverse the final results, leading to a pass and improved results.

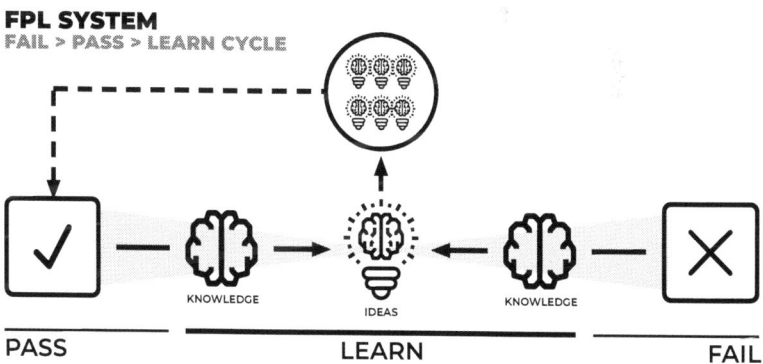

FPL SYSTEM
FAIL > PASS > LEARN CYCLE

PASS   LEARN   FAIL

Figure 24. FPL System (learning cycle)

The FPL system leads to 12 possible outcomes and the decision points that go with them.

Fail Outcomes

1. FAIL: Complete failure discard
   When an experiment is completely unstable, adjustable, or cannot be improved at all.

2. FAIL: Adjustments to pass
   When an experiment has potential, but requires adjustments to improve outcomes

3. FAIL: New idea to pass
   When an experiment has potential, but requires a whole new approach to retest.

Pass Outcomes

4. PASS: Complete pass; go to scale
   When an experiment is a success and can go straight to scaling.

5. PASS: Improve it to make better
   When an experiment is a success, but can use an effective improvement within it.

6. PASS: Add on to it to make better
   When an experiment is a success, and something can be added to make it even better.

Learning Outcomes

7. LEARN – FAIL: Why it didn't work and what to avoid
   When an experiment fails, finding causes that led to failure, and determining how to not repeat them again in
   future experiments.

8. LEARN – FAIL: Why it didn't work and how it can be changed
   When an experiment fails, finding causes that led to
   failure and how small adjustments could improve future
   experiments.

9. LEARN – FAIL: Why it didn't work, but a new better idea
   When an experiment fails, finding causes that led to failure, but a new idea emerges as a solution to be used in
   future experiments.

10. LEARN – PASS: Next is bigger, better ideas to test from
    the start
    When an experiment passes and several new and better
    direct or indirect ideas are generated for future experi-
    ments.

11. LEARN – PASS: Changes or improvements for next level
    When an experiment passes, and adjusts and improve-
    ments can lead to even more successful experiments in
    the future.

12. LEARN – PASS: What elements can be reused in other
    ideas
    When an experiment passes, specific elements that led
    to success can be reused in other ways in future experi-
    ments.

EXERCISE 10: FPL (FAIL, PASS, LEARN) SYSTEM

Start by writing the name of the growth hack itself. Select if it has been a fail or pass; then select the type of fail or pass outcome. Select the learning outcome from the growth hack. Describe in vivid detail what you've learned, but keep the details simple, using a point form approach for easy consumption.

Name of growth hack	☐ **FAIL** ☐ **PASS**
FAIL OUTCOMES ☐ 1. FAIL: Complete failure discard ☐ 2. FAIL: Adjustments to pass ☐ 3. FAIL: New idea to pass	**PASS OUTCOMES** ☐ 4. PASS: Complete pass go to scale ☐ 5. PASS: Improve it to make better ☐ 6. PASS: Add on to it to make better
LEARNING OUTCOMES ☐ 7. LEARN – FAIL: Why didn't it work, and what to avoid ☐ 8. LEARN – FAIL: Why didn't it work, but can be changed ☐ 9. LEARN – FAIL: Why didn't it work, but a new better idea	**LEARNING OUTCOMES** ☐ 10. LEARN – PASS: Next bigger, better ideas to test from the start ☐ 11. LEARN – PASS: Changes or improvements for next level ☐ 12. LEARN – PASS: What elements can be reused into other ideas
Describe the learning outcomes	

Exercise 10. FPL (Fail, Pass, Learn) system

Outcome

This is the final step in the process. There are three main outcomes:

1. YES — Ready to go; let's scale hack
2. RETEST — For strength or adjustment
3. NO — Discard

YES means you're ready to move forward and scale the growth hack itself. RETEST is an interesting outcome where a possible adjustment or improvement may turn something that is a failure into a possible success. The decision is usually based on a hunch that doesn't empirically show up. NO completely discards the experiment outcomes and starts over again.

Not all failures are a waste; it's important to preserve whatever learning can be extracted and recycle it in a fresh and dynamic way. This approach allows for more growth hacking ideas to emerge, giving you a chance to find what can work and eventually scale.

Growth Hacking Extensions

Extended growth hacking is designed to systematically extract more value from your existing experiments (Figure 25). It is about generating new growth hacking ideas based on the current experiments, whether they have failed or passed, and their associated learning.

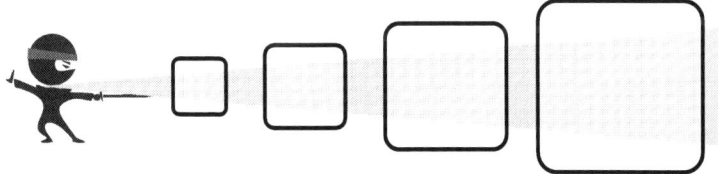

Figure 25. Expanding on existing growth hacks

Growth hack extensions are designed to build on existing momentum to drive creative and practical ways of expanding on what you have already developed.

GROWTH HACK EXTENSIONS
Expanding on failure, success, and learning to discover new growth hacks

Wildcards — Ideas	Adjustments — Ideas	Pain Points — Ideas	Combinations — Ideas
Select an approach and generate ideas.	*Select an adjustment to an existing idea to make a new one.*	*Select a source of pain to generate new ideas.*	*Select a combination approach to generate ideas.*
Select and describe	Select and describe	Select and describe	Select and describe
☐ Adapt from elsewhere ☐ Media scanning ☐ Freestyle	☐ Add ☐ Reduce ☐ Improve ☐ Remove	☐ Customers ☐ Partners ☐ Suppliers	☐ 2 Combinations ☐ 3 Combinations ☐ 4 Combinations

Table 5. Growth hack extensions

Start with existing experiments you have conducted or even ideas you may have generated, but not tested yet. Run them through this step-by-step process. Take all the ideas generated and start testing by using the FPL Growth Hacking Extensions worksheet. The process is:

1. Experiments
2. Wildcards
3. Adjustment
4. Pain Points
5. Combinations
6. New Growth Hacks

1. Experiments

Select either experiments that have failed or passed or ideas that were generated by learning from failures and passes.

EXERCISE 11: EXPERIMENTS FOR GROWTH HACKING EXTENSION
List the experiments, which you have completed, regardless if they are a fail or pass, or newly generated experiments.
List of Experiments to Expand
1
2
3
4
5
6
7
8
9
10

Exercise 11. Experiments for growth hacking extension

2. Wildcards

A wildcard is an event that is unpredictable. Usually we base our analysis on incremental ideas that build on one another, whereas wildcards do not have directly or directly visible link. Consider them something coming out of nowhere but they do exist. Evaluate your experiments, step back, and get creative. There are three ways to generate wild cards.

- Adapting is about finding applications in unrelated areas. You can learn from them and adapt them to your situation.
- Media scanning is discovering new ideas from the media, including social media and online blogs, etc.
- Freestyle incorporates ideas completely generated from scratch; they may not seem relevant at first, but nevertheless may have an impact.

EXERCISE 12: WILDCARD IDEAS TO GENERATE NEW GROWTH HACKS

Develop wildcards from the three categories; think about what can dramatically go wrong (or even right) and the implications. Generate as many ideas as possible. Your objective is to generate solid ideas to experiment with as new growth hacks.

Adapting	Media Scanning	Freestyle

Wildcards from the above categories that you want to experiment with for new growth hacks:

Exercise 12. Wildcard ideas to generate new growth hacks

3. Adjustment

Adjust your experiments by applying one of four approaches to it. First is adding something else that can make it more effective. Second is reducing a part of it to have a new idea. Third is improving either a part or even the whole experiment. Fourth is removing a part to simplify the idea or isolating specific parts that can be adjusted.

EXERCISE 13: ADJUST IDEAS TO GENERATE NEW GROWTH HACKS

Sort your adjustments into four categories that build on existing growth hacks, or even new ideas, where you can apply one of the four techniques. Your objective is to generate solid ideas to experiment with as new growth hacks.

Add	Reduce	Improve	Remove
What can you add to make something better?	*What can you reduce to make something better?*	*What can you improve to make something better?*	*What can you remove to make something better?*

Adjustment ideas from the above categories that you want to experiment with for new growth hacks:

Exercise 13. Adjust ideas to generate new growth hacks

4. Pain Points

Review your experiments and explore three pain points that might be obstacles to new findings. Those three areas are customer pain points, partner pain points, and supplier pain points. Your objective is to dig deeper into these three key areas and see what new growth hacking ideas may emerge.

EXERCISE 14: PAIN POINT IDEAS THAT GENERATE NEW GROWTH HACKS

Sort pain points into three categories; evaluate the big problems they represent where you can add a significant amount of value by solving them. Your objective is to generate solid ideas to experiment with as new growth hacks.

Customers	Partners	Suppliers
Pressing problems that prevent customers from achieving something important	*Pressing problems that prevent partners from achieving something important*	*Pressing problems that prevent suppliers from achieving something important*

Ideas from the above pain point areas that you want to experiment with for new growth hacks:

Exercise 14. Pain point ideas that generate new growth hacks

5. Combinations

Combinations are basically taking more than one existing idea and combining it with another. This can happen in three formats: double, triple, or quadruple combination. Combinations basically allow you to create a cocktail — it either can literally be a mix of two ideas or can spark something completely new by seeing things differently due to new combinations. The purpose of combinations is to stimulate new growth hacking ideas. Note: the fewer the combinations, the simpler the exercise will be; similarly, the more the combinations, the more complex the exercise gets. The idea is to generate new undiscovered areas of potential growth hacks using existing elements.

EXERCISE 15: IDEA COMBINATION TO GENERATE NEW GROWTH HACKS		
Sort combinations into three categories. Think about how these combinations can contribute to generating new idea. Your objective is to generate solid ideas to experiment with as new growth hacks.		
2-combinations	**3-combinations**	**4-combinations**
Bring two completely new ideas together to form a single new idea	Bring three completely new ideas together to form a new idea	Bring four completely new ideas together to form a new idea
Ideas from the combinations above that you want to experiment with for new growth hacks.		

Exercise 15. Idea Combination to generate new growth hacks

6. New Growth Hacks

Review all your wildcards, adjustments, pain points, and combinations. List them in priority order of which ideas you want for experiments. When you decide on which ones to tackle, go back to the FPL experiments and run through the exercise again.

EXERCISE 16: ALL THE EXTENSION GROWTH HACKING IDEAS

Capture the results of wildcards, adjustments, pain points, and combinations below. Then select those that you want to purse as extend growth hacks. At this stage, when you take a top down view, you might generate some new ideas. Capture them below; don't let them disappear.

Wildcards	Adjustment	Pinpoints	Combinations
List your ideas generated from wildcards	*List your ideas generated from adjustments*	*List your ideas generated from pain points*	*List your ideas generated from combinations*

Final selection of ideas for growth hacks to test:

Exercise 16. All the extension growth hacking ideas

The purpose of growth hacking extensions is to stimulate the continuous development of growth hacks. For example, the website booking.com has run a thousand tests a day ever since 1996 to find growth hacks that will boost growth.

Not all of your growth hacking experiments will work. In fact, it's likely that only one or two will turn out to be useful methods. That does not mean the others were a waste of time.

Unfortunately, many companies believe that failure is not an option. If something doesn't work, they give up on the process. But when it comes to growth hacking, failure is a prerequisite for success. No one can tell what will work for your business until you've tried it. Be bold and creative — especially in the beginning.

The FPL system (Fail, Pass, Learn) provides a good way to deal with failures and implement them into your strategy. When you attempt a new strategy, it will either fail or pass. But regardless of the outcome, you can get key takeaways from the experiment.

Even if it doesn't feel like a success, each experiment you make is useful. Thomas Edison noted that he didn't fail 99 times, but instead found 99 ways that didn't work. As an entrepreneur, you need to embrace failure and use it to fuel your next success.

The "learn" part of the FPL system is the most valuable. Failing is only beneficial if you can learn why it happened and correct it for the next time. Unless you can understand why an idea, tool, or tactic didn't work, you're doomed to repeat that failure again down the line.

During the initial phase of a growth hacking campaign, anything goes. You and your team need to be open to new ideas. This is the time when you want to be at your most creative and ambitious.

After the initial push, however, it's time to start cutting the waste from your campaign. Refinement is crucial to long-term success. Effective growth hacking is a process of continuous modification.

To refine your methods you need one thing: data. While the prospectors in your growth hacking team are vital during the experimentation phase, it's the miners who will maintain the momentum as you move forward. Analyzing your data will help you find the most effective methods and allow you to focus your time, energy, and resources on the tactics that work.

> **POWER TIP: Adopt, Drop, or Hop**
>
> *A good way to refine your processes is the Adopt, Drop, or Hop system. Adopt the tools and ideas that work, drop those that fail, and hop to the next idea when you're ready to repeat the process.*

Additional Growth Hacking Methods

Remember: growth hacking methods are not always long-term. Some campaigns will fizzle out regardless of your efforts, which is why hopping to the next idea or experiment is a fundamental part of the process.

Small

Trial and error is an integral part of growth hacking at the beginning, so make your experiments small. Not everything you try will work. Minimize the effect of your failures by keeping your tests at a manageable size.

Travel supergiant booking.com makes up to a thousand tiny tests every day, making it easy to learn which marketing methods work and to avoid wasting time and money on those that don't. These bite-size experiments are not only simpler and easier to control, but are also more measurable, providing more accurate results. Testing for five different objectives at once would make it impossible to know which method tipped the outcome whereas freezing four and isolating one ensures you get meaningful results that are easily analyzed.

Small doesn't have to mean shortsighted. By making simple experiments that provide immediate results, you'll move forward at surprising speed. It can take very little time to make big changes. You can still think long term with short-term experiments by getting the results you need now and bringing them into the context of long-term growth. To get results that scale and sustain, view growth hacking as a journey, not a destination.

> **POWER TIP: The smaller the better**
>
> *If you cannot explain your experiment in 60 seconds to someone who knows nothing about what you do, it's too big. Additionally, the person you explain it to should be able to give constructive feedback, even at a basic level. If it gets too complex to explain and have a conversation with someone, it's already too big to work with.*

Quick

As well as keeping your experiments small, try to keep them quick. Speed is vital if you want to be competitive, stay motivated and make the most of your time and effort.

The market conditions for your product are changing. Consumer behavior and the needs of your customers are constantly evolving. You need to stay flexible and responsive if you want to overtake your competitors. Make sure your experiments take hours or days — not weeks or months — so you get meaningful data that allows you to move in line with your niche.

Longer experiments are also a drain on energy. Keep your team motivated by staying light on your feet and constantly coming up with new ideas.

Finally, remember your capacity. You have only so much time, money, and energy to devote to growth hacking experiments. Favoring quick tests over longer projects will allow you to complete experiments before moving on to the next. As a guide, take a look at the following times required for average growth hacking experiments. These times are based on a team with 4–5 people who have the necessary tools already in place:

- 1 variable experiment — 1–5 hours
- 2–5 variable experiments — 5–10 hours
- 6–10 variable experiments — 15–20 hours

> **POWER TIP: The 20-Minute Tool Test**
>
> Here's a quick way of testing tools for a growth hacking experiment. Organize a team of three people. Now take the top three tools and set a limit of 20 minutes to get

the tool set up, working, and executing an initial result. It doesn't matter if this result isn't high impact; the aim is to get the tool working and assessed for compatibility. Compare the three tools to find the best one for your experiment.

Cheap

The point of growth hacking is to develop and conduct many experiments. Make sure you manage the costs of the tests you make. Set an overall budget in advance and divide it by the number of experiments you want to conduct in a week. As a guide, this weekly number should be:

- 1–25 if you're a recent startup
- 26-49 if you're in the early stages of starting up (preparing to scale-up)
- 50–150 if you're in the later stages of starting up (scaling-up)
- 150–500 if you're already scaling

Remember that every experiment you do will lead to new learning and more unplanned experiments that may require additional money and time. Take this additional investment into account when you budget. Allow leeway for 3–5 new experiments to arise from each test you do. The unpredictability of growth hacking is all the more reason to keep each experiment as cheap as possible.

You may also find that the experiments you conduct in turn need further experiments to fine-tune the results. For every promising result, you'll easily find 15–25 new sub-experiments to get clearer and more in-depth data you can use in your marketing strategy.

Keeping the cost of experiments low is a vital part of growth hacking. Once you find something that works, you'll want to invest in it. Make sure you're realistic about your budget and remember this is just the start.

> **POWER TIP: Capture Your Costs**
>
> *Accurately capture all costs and monitor overtime so you can compare the return on investment for each of your experiments. You don't need to focus on complex costing equations; just get the main costs right. Having a consistent measure will ensure you can make a real comparison.*

Some Dos and Don'ts for Growth Hacking Experiments

When setting out with your growth hacking experiments, it's just as helpful to know what not to do as it is to know what will work. Here are some dos and don'ts to ensure you get the most out of your early experiments:

Do

1. Experiment with tactics.
2. Focus attention and resources on what's working.
3. Invite feedback from users at all stages.
4. Look at analytics and data.
5. Be decisive.

Don't

1. Don't put too much money into one resource.
2. Don't spend too long on one tactic or idea.
3. Don't ignore data, especially churn rates.

4. Don't hesitate on an idea.
5. Don't worry about long-term strategies (yet).

At the beginning, growth hacking is about trying different tactics to see what works. During this phase, the prospectors on your team are going to be the most valuable, as they will be experimenting and finding different ways to promote your product and brand.

There are no wrong answers at this stage. Some tactics won't work, but now is the time to attempt as many different options as possible. As long as you have a robust process of analytics in place, you can refine your process later.

Summary

In this chapter, we reviewed the full growth hacking cycle by going through the three phases that make a growth hack work:

1. Growth **problem** (Exercises 1–4)
   Growth Area, Challenge, Issue, and Ideas

2. Growth hacking **experiments** (Exercises 5–10)
   OKR, Tools, Growth Hack, FPL (Fail, Pass, Learn) System and Outcome

3. Growth hacking **extensions** (Exercises 11–16)
   Wildcard, Adjustments, Pain Points, and Combinations

This cycle helps you master the core of growth hacking, which is experimentation. This systematic approach allows you to run experiments live while reading the chapter, then repeating over and over again through your growth cycles. The objective here is to find the best growth hacks, use them, and then build on them.

CHAPTER NOTES

CHAPTER NOTES

Chapter 5.
Growth hack: and scale your approach

MIND   READY   SET   **Growth hack**   BONUS

In this chapter:

- How to use the *FPL system* for growth hacking
- How to *systemize your processes* for hyper-growth
- How to build on your success *and go beyond*

> **KEY TAKEAWAY:**
> **If the purpose of growth hacking is to grow, you need to use the methods you've learned to turn one experiment into many. Scaling your business relies on learning from your analytics, systemizing your approach, and automating your processes.**

Now that you've learned the basic system for experimenting with growth hacks, it's time to turn the theory into growth. To convert data into tangible growth, you'll need to understand what works and what doesn't, then use that knowledge to refine your marketing process. By systemizing and automating these processes, you'll be able to take your business to the next level. But first, you need to turn your learning into processes.

If you are not scalable, you cannot grow. You may have the best product or service in the world. Yet if demand pushes you to the edge and you cannot deliver to the customer, you never planned correctly to scale. Without planning to scale, your growth is literally doomed. Scale is something you discover with time — it's how you systematically manage growth.

1. Map our future into scale points (volume over time) so you see where you're going.
2. Attract investment, suppliers, and partners who enable your growth.
3. Manage risks from a proactive perspective.
4. Increase profitability while gaining market share.
5. Lower the cost of operations, customer acquisition, and retention.

Understanding Scalability

There are three classifications of scalability: scalable, semi-scalable, and non-scalable.

1. Scalable refers to elements that can be scaled, but have not been scaled yet.
2. Semi-scalable products and services have parts that are scalable and parts that are not; they need to be combined to become scalable.
3. Non-scalable refers to parts that need to be completely transformed into scalable elements in your organization.

There are three characteristics to ensure you are scalable.

1. Repeatability: Do you have a set of actions that can be duplicated?
2. No distortion: As you repeat, do quality and value stay consistent?
3. Longevity: The lifespan must be long-term, not short-term.

If your systems and process cannot be repeated without distortion in the context of a long-time span, you will not be able to scale. At the core of scalability is automation, which are systems that have processes that allow automate execution of repeated routines, while supporting and driving non-routine processes.

Scaling Growth Hacks

In order for growth hacks to work effectively, they have to be sustainable and scalable. For that to happen, they need to be automated. Automation and scaling are arts of their own (Figure 26). They must be mastered to ensure growth hacks work. If a growth is short lived, then it's not worth even attempting. You need growth hacks that can boost aggregate growth; scale and automation are it will happen.

SCALING AND AUTOMATING
GROWTH HACKS

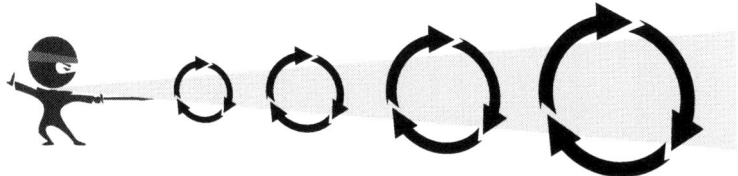

Figure 26. Scaling and automating growth hacks

You should evaluate and develop five key areas for scaling a growth hack (Figure 26). It's important to note though automation is central to your ability to scale. Without powerful automation, scalability becomes less possible.

- *Test for scalability* — Does it work or not?
- *Fail* — If it fails, what else can be done?
- *Automation* — What is the state of the automation capability?
- *Automation strategy* — What is the best approach to automate?
- *Automation considerations* — How can you ensure your automation strategy works?

When bringing these five factors all together, you should be able to differentiate between what can and cannot work, focus on those elements that work, and scale them by making strategic and systemic decisions.

SCALING AND AUTOMATING GROWTH HACK
How to scale and automate growth hacks

Test for Scalability	Failt	Automation	Automation Strategy	Automation Considerations
All hacks must pass all three scalability tests.	If it fails, what are your next options?	Current status of automation	Choose an automation strategy.	How to fine tune your automation strategy
Select	Select	Select	Select	Rank
☐ Repeatable ☐ No distortion ☐ Longevity	☐ Discard ☐ Redesign/ Retest ☐ Do ahead anyways	☐ Not automated ☐ Semi-automated ☐ Fully automated	☐ Build ☐ Outsource ☐ Connect	Costs Time Capabilities Bottlenecks

Table 6. Scaling and automating growth hacks

Test for Scalability

There are three tests that determine if a growth hack is scalable or not: repeatability, no distortion, and longevity Figure 27).

SCALABILITY
TEST

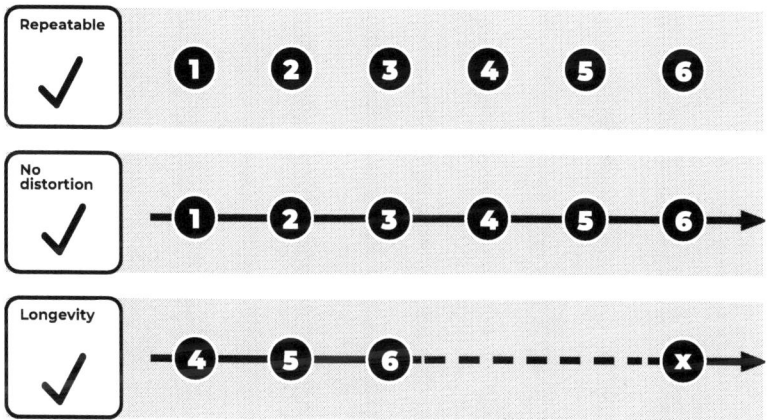

Figure 27. Scalability test

Repeatable

When activities are executed 10, 100, 1000, and even a million times, can they be repeated exactly as when they were executed the first time? If they cannot, then the growth hack fails the repeatable test. If they can, the growth hack passes.

No Distortion

As you repeat, there needs to be no distortion. This means there can be no decline in quality or value when repeating. Ideally there would be an improvement. If there is no distortion, the growth hack passes; if not, it fails.

Longevity

The lifespan of the repeatable and non-distorted process must be long if sustainable and scalable growth is to happen. If the growth hack has a long life span, it passes; if not, it fails.

EXERCISE 17: THE SCALABILITY TEST

List your growth hacks. Test them against the three requirements defined above; then state if it fails or passes. If it fails, you can decide what to do next.

Growth Hack	Test	Pass	Fail
List the growth hacks you're scaling.	*The growth hack must meet all three requirements.*	*Can it scale or not?*	*It failed.*
	☐ Repeatable	☐ Fail >	☐ Discard
	☐ No distortion	☐ Pass	☐ Redesign/Retest
	☐ Longevity		☐ Do ahead anyways
	☐ Repeatable	☐ Fail >	☐ Discard
	☐ No distortion	☐ Pass	☐ Redesign/Retest
	☐ Longevity		☐ Do ahead anyways
	☐ Repeatable	☐ Fail >	☐ Discard
	☐ No distortion	☐ Pass	☐ Redesign/Retest
	☐ Longevity		☐ Do ahead anyways
	☐ Repeatable	☐ Fail >	☐ Discard
	☐ No distortion	☐ Pass	☐ Redesign/Retest
	☐ Longevity		☐ Do ahead anyways
	☐ Repeatable	☐ Fail >	☐ Discard
	☐ No distortion	☐ Pass	☐ Redesign/Retest
	☐ Longevity		☐ Do ahead anyways

Exercise 17. The scalability test

Fail

When scalability fails, there are three ways to manage it. First is to completely discard the growth hack, second is a redesign (which is an adjustment to see if it can pass), and third is to proceed even if it fails, but with caution.

- *Discard*
  The hack will not work at all. It's best just to discard it entirely.
- *Redesign and retest*
  If there is the opportunity for making adjustments that can lead to a pass, it would be worthwhile redesigning and retesting it.
- *Go ahead anyways*
  This is a pure judgment call, but based on a rationale for proceeding even though it has failed; you believe there is still some possibility of it working.

Once a failure for scale happens, it is advisable to discard it and focus efforts on a more scalable growth hack altogether.

Automation

The current systems you have in place or are planning to build will be in one of the following three situations with regard to automation.

- *Not automated*
  Either you have existing systems and processes, but they are not automated, or you may completely lack systems and process altogether.
- *Semi-automated*
  You have existing systems and process where some of them or portions of them are automated, but collectively they are not connected or automated.

- *Full automated*
  Your systems and processes are all automated and connected; both internal and external systems are synchronized together.

If you are not automated, you need to find ways to automate your systems and processes. If you are semi-automated, then focus on becoming completely automated. If you are fully automated, you may be ready for scaling. If the situation cannot be automated or even semi-automated, you need to move towards full automation.

Automation Strategy

Building, outsourcing, and connecting are the three primary strategies for automating. Automation strategies are developed with great systems that have clear, effective, and efficient processes. However, these three primary strategies have 12 subsets that are actionable based on your current and target automation strategy:

1. **Build**
   Entirely build your own systems internally on your own.

   2. Build + Outsource
      Build your primary systems internally, but outsource portions.
   3. Build + Outsource + Connect
      Build your primary systems internally and outsource portions, while connecting with third-party tools.
   4. Build + Connect
      Build your primary systems internally and connect them with third-party tools that enhance your internal systems.

5. Outsource
Entirely outsource your primary systems to be developed externally.

6. Outsource + Build
Outsource your primary system externally, but build internal capacity so that you can eventually build your own.

7. Outsource + Build + Connect
Outsource your primary system externally, while building capacity and utilizing third part tools in the process.

8. Outsource + Connect
Outsource your primary system while blending them with third part tools.

9. Connect
Connecting and using third party tools to automate.

10. Connect + Build
Connecting third-party tools for internal automation systems.

11. Connect + Build + Outsource
Connecting third-party tools with internal automation systems and outsourcing parts.

12. Connect + Outsource
Connecting third-party tools and outsourcing automation systems development.

Automation Considerations

There are four primary considerations when automating:

1. Costs
2. Time
3. Capabilities
4. Bottlenecks

In the case of costs, time, and capabilities, you need sufficient resources in balance with each other when setting up, operating, and growing your automation systems. In the case of bottlenecks when scaling, consider constraints when hitting different scalability points. How will they affect automation to ensure there is no bottleneck in the automation of primary systems?

Make Automation Work

In addition to building a system for your growth hacking process, if you want to achieve hyper-growth, you'll need to make as much of the process happen without you as possible. We looked earlier at how to use tools for automation. There is also a comprehensive list of suitable tools in the Growth Hacker's Toolkit at the end of the book.

Automating as many processes as you can will free you up to focus on new growth hacking strategies. It will also allow your business to scale quickly and efficiently. If the growth hacking strategies you've discovered work only with your input, there will always be a limit to what your business can become.

Choose the automation practices that give you the best results for your business, As a guide, it's a good idea to focus on email management, drip marketing (a sequence of content that drives a customer's interest towards revenue) , managing and analyzing customer data, and Customer Relationship Management (CRM).

By automating as many of these processes as possible, you'll find smart ways to make your growth hacking experiments quicker, easier, and cheaper.

Learn from the FPL System

In Chapter 3, we learned how to use the Fail, Pass, Learn system (FPL) to refine our approach to growth hacking experiments. Refining the process in this way allows you to identify which methods work for your business. But how do you put these into practice?

In Chapter 4, Exercise 4-10: FPL (Fail, Pass, Learn) System), we covered how to turn your learning from the FPL system into effective processes and habits in your business. Knowing what works on a small level can influence how you do things in a big way — and this will lead to growth.

Once you've learned from your experiments and converted your learning into ideas, habits, and rules within your business, it's time to speed up the growth process.

Most businesses grow by using sensible marketing strategies over a long period of time. However, to achieve fast growth on a significant scale, you'll need some way of accelerating this process. This is where growth hacking comes into its own. Once you've conducted some experiments and tried different methods, you need to turn your attention to implementing what works on a larger scale. The two major components in turning growth hacking experiments into real-life growth are systemization and automation.

Since we have covered automation, the next step is systemization. Systemization allows you to optimize your automation. For example, you may be collecting basic customer information, but not behavioral data like how often they visit your website or store. By automating the collection and analysis of that data, you can now systemize how you can further incentivize revisting customers by giving them exclusive offers.

Systemization

The beginning of your growth hacking journey has been all about coming up with different ideas. Since we're still in the early stages, ideation and experimentation are going to remain the core components of the process. However, as growth hacking becomes a part of your long-term marketing strategy, a system for implementing your ideas will allow you to use them more effectively (Figure 28).

You can look at systemization in three levels:

1. **Non-routine,**
   Activities that are not performed frequently but are non-vital
2. **Routine,**
   Activities that are performed frequently
3. **Unique activities**
   Vital activities not performed frequently

SYSTEMIZATION
OF PROCESSES

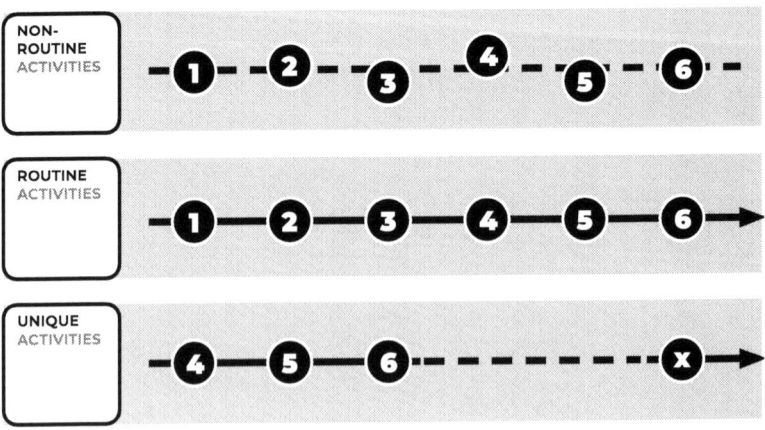

Figure 28. Systemization of processes

Although growth hacking is based on experimentation, you can still be organized and systematic in your approach. Running experiments in a controlled system allows you to track the results more easily, make adjustments more quickly, and still retain the creativity needed to think of new ideas.

Turning growth hacking into a system will also give you some wider benefits. Not least of these is that everyone on your team will understand where they fit and how they can help push the company forward. It's much easier to work together when everyone knows the rules.

You'll also be able to scale more quickly. True growth occurs when you have measurable OKRs and your experiments are conducted within a defined structure. If they're not, your company's growth will be patchy and you'll find it impossible to focus your attention on the results you want.

Growth Hacking Structure

Let's look at how you can define and maintain a growth hacking structure that will help your business scale.

Conduct More Experiments

Once you have a rough foundation for your growth hacks, it will be easier to run additional experiments and see what works (Figure 29). When your team works together with defined OKRs in mind, it's much easier for individuals to share new ideas. These ideas will bounce off each other, build, and grow organically, leading to further experimentation and new learning.

Remember also that the more experiments you conduct, the more audiences you'll reach. Methods that work for one group of people won't work for others; therefore, come up with different ways to expand your user base.

MORE EXPERIMENTS
LEAD TO MORE LEARNING AND BIGGER BETTER
IDEAS FOR GROWTH HACKS

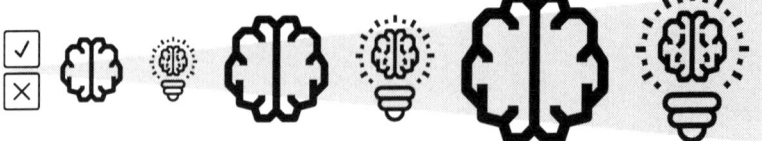

Figure 29. Conducting more experiments

2 Reasons Making More Experiments Leads to Growth

When you experiment, you can create better growth and success for your business. Here's why:

1. *Your Audience Changes*. What works for early adopters probably won't attract the general population? Continuing to make more experiments allows you to account for these differences and move with your audience.
2. *Each Hack Has Expiration*. No matter how successful, any experiment will fizzle out eventually. This paves the way for new ideas and allows you to discover new hacks along the way.

Ensure Each Experiment Feeds into the Next

If you want your experiments to create long-lasting success, it's important to make sure that each one feeds into another. Instead of testing a large number of ideas at once and seeing what sticks, experiment within a defined framework so that each new idea leads into an improved version.

For example, if you want to increase the number of downloads of your app from 0 to 100, you might try including a link for current users to share with friends. If you then find that a link isn't incentive enough for users to promote the app, you might decide to offer a bonus for people who do promote it.

Working off this idea, you then decide to add another incentive by making the app more sociable. You add a feature that allows users to interact with friends within the app, encouraging people to share and promote it more readily.

Note how important the OKR is in this example. Without the objective in place, it would be easy to lose sight of what you're trying to achieve. By defining the OKR *before* you put it to the test, you're able to start small and build. Because all the experiments are geared towards a single objective (increasing user downloads), it's much easier to keep them structured and focused.

Make Habits Out of Experiments

One reason why growth hacking fails is that teams lose sight of the need for constant experimentation. While ideation is at its most valuable in the early stages, it shouldn't be the only time you do it. Instead, make a habit out of experimenting. Test new concepts all the time, even if your growth exceeds expectations. Growth stalls when we rest on our laurels and assume that what we're doing is enough.

As we discussed in previous chapters, your growth team should be comprised of both prospectors and miners. Because both of these types of team members are great at a particular aspect of growth hacking (experimentation and refinement, respectively), you can use them to your advantage.

Have the prospectors on your team continue to come up with new ideas throughout the process and test them.

Meanwhile, have the miners work on those ideas that have already proven successful. Creating this kind of system will ensure that you always maintain momentum and that you can adapt to changing circumstances.

Review, Analyze, and Adjust

We've already seen the vital role analysis and refinement play in growth hacking experimentation. To make your techniques as efficient as possible, build analytics into your system and ensure you review it regularly. For each new experiment, make you should have a process in place to analyze the data that comes out of it.

Use the miners on your team for this effort, and remember: you can't refine your process unless you know what works.

The need for constant review and analysis will also have an impact on the tools you use. Whenever you decide to conduct a new experiment, make sure you have the tools in place to measure its effectiveness. If you're unable to track its success, how will you tell if it worked?

One issue that can arise when measuring success is that it's difficult to know which metrics are being influenced by a particular tactic. If you have several ideas working simul-taneously — for example, three different promotions to get users to sign up — you'll need to break down the perfor-mance of each one so you can refine your methods accor-dingly. If you only see the number of new users increase, how can you determine which tactic is having the most impact?

Establishing a growth hacking process will help you to eliminate any tactic that isn't working. Have a threshold for results so you can make that decision easily — for example, if you're running three experiments to increase user downloads, cut any method that isn't generating a 5% increase. You can use the same threshold for longer experiments too. A marketing method might have had incredible success at first, but for various reasons proves to be unsustainable. By establishing a threshold, you can eliminate any method as soon as it stops producing the desired result.

As with all marketing, growth hacking shouldn't be seen as a short-term boost to your brand. You might experience the most rapid growth when you still have unlimited potential, but even companies that have immense market share can find new and different ways to grow.

For this reason, don't just build a foundation for growth hacking to get instant results. Also develop a framework that enables long-term success.

Build Longevity

Successful growth hacking depends not only on refining each idea as you test and measure it, but also creating a systematic growth hacking system in its own right. As you hone your strategy, you should end up with a lean structure you can use as you grow your business.

Once you have this process down, it will become infinitely easier to continue your success well into the future. As you expand your brand, you'll be able to utilize the same tools and methods to increase your market share, as well as customer retention and satisfaction.

5 Ways to Ensure This Process Is a Success

No matter how fast you grow, you should always be experimenting and finding new ways to reach new markets and customers. In short, hacking never stops. Here are five ways to ensure future experimentation.

1. *Have Ideation Meetings Regularly.* Whether it's each month or each quarter, bring the team together for new growth hacking ideas.
2. *Create a Minimum Number of Ideas.* As an example, make sure that you always have five more hacks in development at all times.
3. *Create an Ideation Department.* Once your company reaches a certain size, assign growth hacking to a specific team.
4. *Check Progress Quarterly.* Be sure to check in on your hacking group to see how well they are performing.
5. *Use Experimentation Worksheets (FPL).* Document successes and failures along the way for posterity and so that you can draw inspiration when ideas are running dry.

Constraints

Anyone running a startup knows that, in the real world, there are constraints that prevent you from achieving growth. Whether you're short of time, team members, money, or other resources to build a successful growth hacking campaign, you'll need to think of ways to get around these limitations.

Time

Growth hacking can be a time-consuming process. Lack of time to set up experiments, manage their execution, and analyze the data they produce is one of the reasons growth hacking fails. Manage your time by making experiments small and quick. Avoid lengthy tactics that can't be analyzed easily. By starting small and choosing your tools wisely, you'll avoid wasting time on experiments that don't work.

Team Members

Startups often have limited resources when it comes to staff; use your existing team members wisely. Assess individuals' skills to see how you can use them in different experiments. If you have a team member who can build compelling landing pages, don't waste them on email management.

Money

Most startups operate on a shoestring, which is all the more reason to make your experiments cheap to run. Use the same tool for more than one process. Think carefully before investing in expensive tools you might not need. Remember: the expensive online tools are not always the best and there are often basic free versions that will do everything you need it to.

Mindset

The mindset of an organization sets its culture. If the culture is open and collaborative, then better results will emerge. Shaping a culture of risk taking, openness, willingness to see the world differently, and action are just a few characteristics that help create a growth mindset. If office politics, silos, and bureaucracy challenge your organization, your results will reflect this. Leaders need to shift the mindset by shaping a new culture that enables growth not stop it.

Skill Set

If you don't have the right talent with the right attitude, growth will be challenging. You need a mix of technical, business, and creative talent. The skill sets need to be deep, yet broad enough to tackle a variety of problems. In making this work, the attitudes of your talent force have to be open, collaborative, and willing to take risks in a team setting.

Build on Success

The key to scaling your business is to take any success and build on it until you have a system that works in a wider context. The time will come, however, when you'll need to step outside of what you've been doing so far. We've already seen how your OKRs will change according to your business needs. At first, your goals will be based solely on building brand identity and recognition. However, once you become well known, your objective will be to increase the value of each user.

Growth will then come in a variety of areas, but here are the three main ways you'll be able to scale your business: expanding into new markets, offering new features, and offering new products.

Expand into New Markets

A new market can mean a new geographic location or a different demographic. For example, you might already appeal to male teenagers aged 14–19 but want to increase that appeal to male adults aged 20–30. Perhaps your product or service is located in a particular city, but you might want to expand into new territories.

The ride-sharing platform Uber might seem ubiquitous. However, when it started, it operated in just one city:

San Francisco. In order to scale, it would have to replicate its success in another city, then another, until it became synonymous with reliable taxi services worldwide. So how did Uber turn one city (2009) into 600 (2019)?

Uber replicated its success by acting not as a single startup, but as many startups under one umbrella. Every time it targeted a new location, it would act as if it was starting from scratch. Except for one difference: each time they did this, they had more knowledge about what worked and what didn't. Although each city was different, Uber had worked out how to grow in one location, then tweaked and refined that process until it had a protocol for growth.

This protocol is now used whenever Uber expands into a new market. The process has to adapt to different cultures and market conditions, but the principles are the same. Behind it all is a rigorous process of testing and refinement.

Expansion into new markets has its challenges. What works with one demographic won't necessarily have the same impact on a different group. The beauty of growth hacking is that you can adjust your strategy accordingly while keeping the structure of your process the same.

Offer New Features

As you try to appeal to both new and current users, your product will likely undergo some transformations. For example, if you're selling an app, you might add new features that make it more user-friendly while also appealing to new customers.

When you think about adding new features to your product, use the data you collect from your growth hacks to make informed decisions about what will work best. Avoid sudden overhauls; these can cause a backlash among your existing users and be disastrous if done wrong. Change is received best when it's implemented incrementally, so avoid reinventing the wheel.

Offer New Products

Although your initial product may have been a success, you will reach a limit in its development. If your product is an app, each customer will download it only once, so think about expanding your brand with new products. As long as you adhere to the overall mission statement of your company, you don't have to be a one-trick pony. Then, as new products come out, you can utilize the same growth hacking methods to expand your user base, this time including those who already use your product.

Each of these methods for expansion will help you maintain momentum and grow your business. By putting a system for growth hacking in place, you'll ensure you scale quickly and efficiently.

Keep up to Date with Growth Hacking

Growth hacking is a changing market, so you have to be sure that you're keeping up with new ideas and trends into the future. Here are some great resources for you to use.

- *Growthhackers.com* — This is a community of hackers and the prime resource for any changes to the industry.
- *Hubspot.com* — Inbound marketing is the bread and butter of this site, and it's always at the forefront of changing trends and dynamics.
- *Neilpatel.com* — Patel is an industry leader; he breaks down these fluctuations in an easy-to-understand format.

- *Growthtools.io* — This site provides a comprehensive list of growth hacking tools by category, with a guide to costs.
- *DreamGrow.com* — This site is a good source of free content marketing resources and a list of growth hacking tools.
- *GrowWithWard.com* — Ward van Gasteren is a growth consultant and growth hacking expert who offers up-to-date information on his site.

Summary

In this chapter, we have looked at how to extend growth hacks by scaling them. Without a growth hack being scalable, it will not have legs. At the core of a scalable growth hack is automation, which enables growth. We have covered:

1. How to evaluate, qualify, and develop scalability
2. How to embrace automation and build an automation strategy
3. How to identify and manage constraints and build success form there

Only when a growth hack is scaled and automated will you realize the full breadth of benefits of that hack itself. Scale and automation keep it cost effective, constant, and measurable for adjustments with time.

CHAPTER NOTES

CHAPTER NOTES

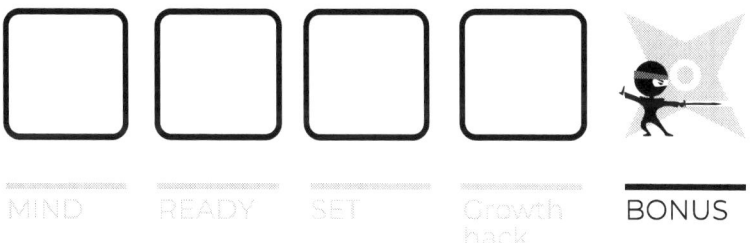

MIND   READY   SET   Growth   **BONUS**
                                    hack

Hire a Growth Hacker

Understanding the concept of growth hacking is one thing, but putting these ideas into action is another. As a startup, you probably don't have a ton of resources at your disposal, but one thing is certain: you're going to need help.

No matter how talented you are, you can't grow your business by yourself. Even if you can get the ball rolling, once your efforts are yielding results, you'll need some assistance. Growth hacking works best when you have a team behind you. Building that growth team is a big step in preparing to scale. In this chapter, we'll discuss ways to bring top growth hackers to your startup and how to utilize them efficiently, particularly if you're short on resources.

***Growth hackers** are a unique breed of talent. They bring many skill sets into a single touch point. Their main characteristics that bring them together is their ability to drive everything they do and work on towards growth — not marketing or any other specific function only, as they exclusively focus on growth only*

Growth Hackers Skill Set Map

The growth hackers skill set map has four core areas summarizing the kinds of skills that growth hackers need. These areas are strategy, revenue development, outreach capability, and optimization skills. Ideally, growth hackers will have a mix of these skills, with a range of coverage across as many of them as possible. When creativity and execution are combined with these skills, talented growth hackers can achieve great results. They don't need to be in-depth experts in all areas. However, they will have selected areas of expertise be able to cover all these areas effectively.

Covering all these areas effectively doesn't mean executing on all of them. Growth hackers need to manage them in a balanced, yet effective manner. At the core of growth hacking is experimentation. To successfully manage an experiment, you will need a breadth of integrated skills — not isolated ones — that will optimize your work and also enhance your ability to scale quickly.

SKILL SET MAP

GROWTH HACKERS SKILL SET MAP

STRATEGIC DEVELOPMENT	REVENUE DEVELOPMENT	OUTREACH DEVELOPMENT	OPTIMIZATION DEVELOPMENT
▪ Behavioral psychology ▪ Storytelling ▪ Research ▪ Design UI/UX	▪ Data and analytics ▪ Branding and positioning ▪ Copywriting ▪ Content creation ▪ A/B testing ▪ HTML, CSS, JavaScript, PHP, etc. ▪ Customer experience	▪ Public relations ▪ Community development ▪ Social media engagement ▪ Business development ▪ Email marketing ▪ Customer relationship management	▪ Operational process optimization ▪ Conversion rate optimization ▪ Search engine optimization

Table 7. Growth Hacker Skill set map

What to Look for in Growth Hackers

One of the problems facing startups trying to build a growth team is the large number of self-proclaimed growth hackers who don't actually know the first thing about growth hacking.

A quick search online will reveal hundreds of marketers who say they specialize in growth hacking. However, when it comes to implementing an effective growth strategy, they fall short. How do you separate the wannabes from the legitimate hackers who can take your startup to the next level? Here are some things to watch out for.

Prospector or Miner?

An analogy many marketers use when evaluating growth hackers is whether they are prospectors or miners. Let's break down the differences between the two.

Prospector

Prospectors are all about experimentation and discovery. They love finding new tools and seeing how they can use them to grow your business. Just like a gold prospector, they love digging holes all over the place, trying to find the elusive treasure.

Best For: Fledgling brands that have little or no current growth

Miner

A miner uses data and analytics to adjust existing marketing tactics so they'll work better. Rather than experimenting (which can lead to failure), a miner will build only upon an existing framework, seeking ways to make it more efficient.

Best For: Companies experiencing rapid growth who need to maintain long-term success

As you can imagine, to get the most out of growth hacking, it's best to have both kinds of hackers on your team: prospectors to discover the best methods for reaching your target audience and miners to capitalize on that growth and ensure its ongoing success. But not all startups have the resources to employ both types of marketer. Invest in the growth hacker that best suits your business stage.

10 Resources for Growth Hacker Recruitment

Getting the right people can make a significant difference in the success and growth of your startup.

Here are 10 places where you might find the best growth hackers.

1. Growthhackers.com — This site is the premier online community of growth hackers.
2. Inbound.org — This site attracts a lot of marketers, including growth hackers.
3. Job Sites — Be sure to include growth hacking in your job description.
4. Online Ads (Craigslist) – Not the best place to find a growth hacker, but you may find some diamonds in the rough.
5. Universities — Contact the alumni department, specifically the people in charge of getting recent grads hired in the field.
6. Recruiters — Let them know what you need from a growth hacker so that they can recruit accordingly.
7. Google Search — Find growth hackers via personal websites and social media pages.
8. LinkedIn — Finding professionals is easy when everyone on LinkedIn is a professional.
9. Reddit — Look for forums related to growth hacking and post your job offer.
10. Marketing Firms — Growth hackers and marketers have similar job descriptions, so this can be an excellent place to start.

Key Phrases to Use When Searching for a Growth Hacker

Doing a Google search for growth hackers can be an excellent way to find the right people for your startup. However, you need to be sure that you're looking for the right characteristics. Here are some key phrases to include in your searches.

KEY PHRASES TO FIND GROWTH HACKERS

▪ Hire a growth hacker	▪ Startup growth hacker	▪ Growth hacker conferences	▪ Growth hacker meet ups
▪ Growth hackers for hire	▪ Growth hacker resume	▪ Influential growth hackers	▪ Growth hacking services
▪ Where to find growth hackers	▪ Freelance growth hackers	▪ Top rated growth hackers	▪ Growth agency
▪ Growth hacker jobs	▪ Need a growth hacker	▪ Growth hackers listed	▪ Growth hacker agency
▪ Top growth hackers	▪ Growth hacker events		▪ Growth hacker agencies
			▪ Growth hacker groups

Table 8. Key phrases searches to find growth hackers

Make sure you talk to any potential hire about their thoughts on growth hacking. Remember: Their true north should be growth. If they're focused on other aspects of marketing, they may not be the right fit.

5 Ways to Engage a Growth Hacker or Freelancer

Unfortunately, most skilled growth hackers will be already working for someone else. That means you may have to settle for hackers with less experience, but don't compromise on knowledge, enthusiasm, or expertise. Here are five considerations when hiring a growth hacker.

1. Technical Expertise. What kind of programs and developing have they done in the past?
2. Work Experience. Even if it's not growth hacking per se, look for any work history you can leverage for growth (e.g., marketing, sales, etc.)
3. Values. What is most important to them? What is their goal with growth hacking?
4. Future Plans. What do they hope to achieve by working with your startup? Build a resume? Long-term career?

Belief in the Product. Talk to them about what your company is selling. Pitch your idea to the growth hackers and see if they get excited about it.

Alignment with your Goals

Anyone you ask to join your team needs to understand your business and be on board with your objectives. Not all growth hackers use the same techniques; some of them will be better suited to your brand than others. If you need someone who can program and create your app based on customer feedback, then you don't want a growth hacker who specializes in making landing pages.

Having clear goals will help you determine the best choice for the position. Lay out your objectives before you start looking for new team members.

Viable Experience

Another thing to look for in a growth hacker is their level of experience, especially with similar companies. If hackers haven't worked on campaigns like yours, how can you expect them to be successful?

When looking at their experience, make sure you look at the specific role they performed on a campaign. What part did the growth hackers play? What were their duties?

Finding Collaborators Inside and Outside Your Organization

Depending on the size of your startup, you may already have people who can help you hack your way to growth. If you have a goal in mind and you know the tools you need to achieve it, you may not have to search for outside talent at all.

Don't assume you'll have to recruit top hackers to make your company stand out. If you have a viable product that can gain traction, you're already in an excellent position to grow rapidly. All you need is the right infrastructure to make that growth sustainable.

How to Recruit Top-Quality Growth Hackers

If you do decide to hire an external growth hacker, you'll want to employ the best you can afford. Although each growth hacker is different, here are some effective ways to cultivate top talent for your business.

Pitch Your Brand or Idea

If customers are already clamoring for your product, it will be easier to get a growth hacker on board. Growth hackers love the thrill of success, so if an idea is promising you'll attract growth hackers willing to invest time and effort into your brand.

> **EXAMPLE**: *Illustrate the traction you have already been able to gain, even if it's not as much as you would*

like it to be. At the same time, be very specific about the challenges you have faced that need to be hacked for growth; tell the story of what things will be like when they are solved.

Talk about Expectations

Before hiring anyone, discuss what you expect of that person as well as what they expect of you. Discussing everything in detail beforehand will eliminate any misunderstandings and help you assess whether your hire is fulfilling their end of the bargain. You'll also be able to measure success and the return on your investment.

When you discuss expectations, talk about your benchmarks for growth as well as pay and bonuses. If you don't have much capital, you may be at a disadvantage, but it doesn't mean you can't recruit great talent. For example, if growth hackers can earn bonuses based on performance, they may be willing to start at a lower salary.

> **EXAMPLE**: *Lay everything out, as it is: the good, the bad, and even the ugly. However, be fair and balanced about getting growth hackers vested into your success. Do consider equity, stock options, and profit sharing. Make it attractive so they are bought into the long-term success of the organization.*

Build a Rapport

People work for people, not companies. However successful your brand, if you don't get along with your growth team, they're likely to go elsewhere. Building a successful team is as much about relationships as expertise, so don't neglect to create rapport between you and the rest of the team.

EXAMPLE: *Bridge the gap when you and any growth hackers by understanding their mindset and practice better. This way you can speak their language and be able to set growth expectations more easily. Always be sure to get their insights on how they see realistic growth hacks working within your context.*

Summary

In this bonus chapter, we looked how to find and engage a growth hacker. It's important to note that a growth hacker is not a digital marketer or just purely a marketing person. Growth hackers are their own unique breeds of talent. We have covered:

1. Growth hackers skill set map
2. Recruitment resources and techniques
3. How to form and leverage internal and external collaboration

Most organizations are likely to start with a freelancer or consultant as a growth hacker, which is a great start. It's important to ensure you engage the long-term vested interest of growth hackers.

CHAPTER NOTES

CHAPTER NOTES

BONUS CHAPTER B:
50 EXAMPLES OF GROWTH HACKING

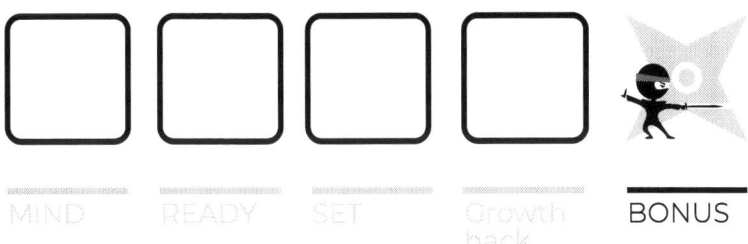

MIND   READY   SET   Growth hack   **BONUS**

Growth hacking is all about finding new shortcuts to success. One of the most valuable activities for your startup is to evaluate methods other companies have used. Not only will this step stimulate your own creativity, it will show you what has worked before. You might not be able to replicate those methods exactly, but they can serve as inspiration for new strategies that could work in your business.

Before we start looking at real-world examples, here are some tips for generating new growth hacking experiments:

Document Ideas

One brainstorming session might generate dozens of strategies, but not all of them will be hits. Document each method from inception to implementation; track its progress to see if it works the way you thought it would. Keeping track of each new idea will help you refine it for future experiments.

Set Goals for Each Method

Remember to set OKRs for each growth hacking technique so you have an idea of what you want to achieve. If you don't quantify both your goals and your progress, it is much harder to focus your attention on what is working best.

Don't Do Too Much at Once

Once you've brainstormed ideas and developed a list of experiments, it's easy to get swept up in the excitement and try to immediately implement as many of them as possible. Instead, it's better to rank your ideas, and then begin with the ones you think will perform the best. As you proceed, you can add new tactics to your growth hacking strategy, building on your momentum.

50 Proven Growth Hacking Examples

To kick start your creativity, here are 50 ways other startups have used growth hacking to their advantage. Use these examples as a springboard to discover potential hacks that could work for your startup. You might not experience their exact results, but you can adopt certain aspects of the strategies to replicate the technique.

The exercise below is designed to help you use the examples in this chapter in your own business. Spend time analyzing how and why they worked, use the following process:

EXERCISE 18: GROWTH HACKING IDEA GENERATION
How to learn from other growth hacks and develop your own

HACK	Apply	Adapt	Better	Combination	IDEAS
Growth hacks	Does this apply?	Adjustments to make this hack idea work for you	Take this hack idea and improve it to better.	Combine hacks to develop new and better ones.	Growth hack idea
Select	YES / NO	Approach and description	Approach and description	Approach and description	List of ideas
	☐ YES ☐ NO	☐ Directly adapt ☐ Remove part(s) and adapt ☐ Improve part(s) or all and adapt	☐ Improve it all ☐ Improve part(s) and make better ☐ Remove part(s) and make better	☐ 2 combinations (Simple) ☐ 3 combinations (intermediate) ☐ 4 combinations (Complex)	1. 2. 3.

Exercise 18. Growth hacking idea generation

Start by working growth hacks from the 50 examples below into this process, which is designed to help you generate new ideas that are suitable to your business and situation. In the left column, list the selected proven growth hacks (from the following examples) that appeal to you the most. Then run them through the process below.

Understand the hack. What was the product? What audience did the hack target? What was the OKR? The more you can understand about the process used, the more you'll be able to use it in your own business.

> **Instructions for Exercise B-1:** If you understand the hack, move to the next step. If not, spend some time to research it before moving forward.

Apply it to your own business. Was the product similar to what you offer? For the most part, growth hacking works well for digital products and services, such as smartphone apps. If your product is significantly different, you will need to extrapolate to get the same result. Now think about the demographics. Who were the companies trying to reach? Do you target the same audience? If so, it will be easier to use the same ideas to come up with a new hack. If your audience is different, it might be best to try a different approach.

> ***Instructions for Exercise B-1:*** *If this doesn't apply to your business, move to the next part. If there might be an indirect association, move to the next step; otherwise, find another hack as an example.*

Adapt it to make it work. In some cases the companies below were able to experience rapid growth only because the right elements came together at the right time. In those instances, you won't be able to repeat that same success. Focus on growth hacks that used a specific methodology and step-by-step system to achieve results. This way, you can follow a similar formula and see how it works for you.

> ***Instructions for Exercise B-1:*** *If you can directly adapt the hack, do so. If not, learn from it to advance, or remove parts you see that might not work well for you and adapt it. You might find parts that need improvement for the hack to be more suitable to your business.*

Improve the hack. What could you do even better? Do you know of a better tool? Could you do it in half the time? Think about how you could make the hack more efficient and effective.

> ***Instructions for Exercise B-1:*** *See if you can improve the whole idea or see if there are parts you can take and improve. Perhaps you can remove parts that may not be needed, then make the hack better.*

Combine the hack with another one. The purpose of growth hacking is to be as streamlined as possible. Could you use the tool or method chosen by the companies below to conduct another hack at the same time? Doubling up will save you time and money.

> *Instructions for Exercise B-1: See how you can combine two, three, or four hacks either to directly create something new or to stimulate new ideas based on those combinations. Remember that a double combination is simple, a triple is intermediate in complexity, and four or more are much more complex. Try to start with simple combinations before taking on more complex ideas.*

Create a growth hack of your own. Having answered the questions above, what's your final idea for a growth hack based on the one you've learned about? Remember to discard any that aren't applicable for your business.

> *Instructions for Exercise B-1: Generate as many high-level ideas here as possible. You can then start the process from scratch in Chapter 4 to feed these new ideas you have gathered from others into your own growth hacks. The purpose here is to generate the ideas, then to take them back to the main process and experiment to see if they can become viable growth hacks or not.*

#1 Shazam

This music app identifies songs using sound-recognition software. Users were encouraged to hold their phones up to speakers at loud venues, such as clubs and music festivals, which sparked a conversation about what they were doing. This growth hack experiment led to over 500 million downloads.

#2 Dollar Shave Club

Dollar Shave Club used viral marketing to promote their brand. They produced a video ad highlighting the service for just $1 per month. The video got 19 million views and helped skyrocket the company's success.

#3 LinkedIn

This massive networking site grew from two to 200 million users by allowing people to create individual public profiles. Because the profiles would show up in Google search results, it helped the site grow exponentially in just a few years.

#4 YouTube

As the second largest search engine behind Google (although Google owns it), YouTube became a household name by allowing users to embed videos on other sites. This directed traffic from millions of pages back to YouTube, increasing its user base to over 1.3 billion.

#5 Quora

Forum sites like Quora have a lot of competition. To increase user retention, they customized the feed based on a person's interests rather than what was trending. The feed became more engaging, so people started relying on this site more than other forums.

#6 Uber

Born in the tech-friendly city of San Francisco, one of Uber's earliest growth hacking techniques was to help organize tech events and then provide free rides for attendees. These events attracted a lot of "early adopter" types, who spread the word. The app went viral soon after.

#7 Dropbox

To encourage users to become brand ambassadors, Dropbox offered free storage to anyone who referred others and connected their account to social media. In this way, the company gamified its referral process (making the experience playful and fun for the user) and now has over 500 million users worldwide.

#8 Bounce Exchange

Having lead pages and CTAs (click through rates) is essential for converting leads into customers. Bounce Exchange took this a step further by adding an opt-in form that sent demos to interested customers. By offering this service, the site increased its user base substantially.

#9 Airbnb

This growth hack is hard to replicate, but it shows that ingenuity can have a significant effect if you know what you're doing. The fledgling site hacked into Craigslist's huge user base to connect with customers searching for places to stay. This tactic helped Airbnb to explode seemingly overnight.

#10 Netflix

When this video rental/streaming service began, it targeted its audience with precision. Netflix posted ads on sites and forums frequented by DVD buyers, offering them an easy way to check out new titles that were hard to find elsewhere. This approach led to massive early growth and helped propel Netflix into the powerhouse it is today.

#11 Facebook

The biggest social media company in the world has used a number of growth hacks on its journey to success, but one of the most prescient was tapping into its users' contact lists. By sending messages to everyone they knew, the site was able to grow exponentially.

#12 Gmail

Although Gmail is now one of the biggest email servers in the world, when it first started, Yahoo and Hotmail were the big players. To compete with its rivals (and preserve its limited storage space), Gmail created an aura of exclusivity, making its service "invite only." This created a buzz by making people feel special about using the platform.

#13 Hotmail

There's a reason that Hotmail was top dog before Gmail came along: every time someone sent an email through the server, a link was added to the bottom: "PS. I love you. Get your free email at Hotmail". When the recipient clicked on the link they were directed to a registration page. The more emails that were sent, the more users signed up.

#14 Groove

Part of Groove's success came from being a pioneer in its industry. It was the first blog about building and running a SaaS (software as a service) company, and the experiences they shared made their content go viral. As a result, they were able to build a substantial user base.

#15 Twitter

When Twitter first started, people would sign up and then quickly lose interest. However, by analyzing data, Twitter discovered that anyone who followed at least 10 people tended to stick around. As a result, they started to encourage new users to follow contacts and suggestions as part of the onboarding process, which increased retention and built a stable user base.

#16 Buffer

This app helps companies manage their social media posting. The founder grew the business from a startup by writing articles and posting them on third-party sites. The goal was to get views and link back to Buffer, so he found out what got lots of traffic and used it as inspiration.

#17 Groupon

This site has a built-in way to encourage new users to sign up. Because a certain number of people have to buy the coupon for it to work, users have an incentive to share the deal.

#18 OkCupid

As a dating site, OkCupid has access to a lot of data about its users. The company used this data to create content such as quizzes, which it shares across various channels. The quizzes not only encourage interaction among users, but supply more data about its customers.

#19 Aweber

Aweber is an email marketing tool that taps into humans as social animals who naturally want to do what other people are doing. Aweber tapped into this psychology by showing who had already signed up and when. This information showed new users that the app was popular and encouraged them to sign up themselves.

#20 Hubspot

This hack shows that becoming an authority in your field can help you gain traction. Content marketing site Hubspot offered a free website grader, which would show users how useful their website is. The tool led back to the Hubspot site, where people would see that they had more to offer.

#21 Harvest Snaps

As we've seen, FOMO (fear of missing out) marketing can be highly effective. Healthy snack provider Harvest Snaps tapped into this by offering an exclusive membership club for subscribers, which helped users feel like they were part of something special. This exclusivity spurred others to join as well.

#22 Spotify

Music app Spotify boosted its audience by integrating with Facebook. Tapping into such an extensive market by allowing users to share on the platform increased its audience and grew it into a super-brand.

#23 Paddy Power

Notoriety can help a startup gain traction quickly. Online betting site Paddy Power boosted its online presence by performing high-profile stunts on social media. One example was promising to carve "C' mon England" in the Amazon rainforest ahead of the Rio World Cup. All publicity is good publicity.

#24 Instagram

Sometimes, simplicity is all you need for growth. Instagram relied on creating an intuitive and user-driven site to hack its way to growth. By creating an excellent product that was free to download, it became one of the most-used social media, creative sharing sites in the world.

#25 PayPal

Like Airbnb, PayPal, an online payment provider, used an existing network to build an audience. By collaborating with eBay and using automated robots (bots) to buy items, it boosted its profile on the site. As users noticed PayPal more and more, they started to adopt it, turning the company into the worldwide powerhouse it is today.

#26 ALS "Ice Bucket Challenge"

Although this hack wasn't for a company, it shows how social media can drive awareness and, in this case, raise enormous funds for the battle against the disease ALS. The campaign worked by creating a challenge that people would want to participate in to get likes and views. It then asked participants to nominate others to take the challenge as well. This combination led to an international phenomenon that virtually everyone heard about.

#27 Skype

A communication program like Skype — a free, online calling and messaging service that enables users to have face-to-face conversations from remote distances — only works if you have people to talk to, which requires them to have Skype themselves. The platform made users invite their friends and contacts, creating an endless promotional loop.

#28 The Body Coach

In some cases, flooding the market is a great way to increase exposure. Joe Wicks (the Body Coach — a health transformation solution) promoted his business by posting before and after pictures of his clients on numerous social media sites. Over time, he gained a following and built a reputation.

#29 Monzo

Being first in line for a new product can feel pretty good, which is why Monzo grew so fast. The online banking company showed how many people were in front of you to download the app, and how many were behind you. You could "jump" the line by referring others. Because people have a natural desire to be first, they made referrals to get ahead of others.

#30 Zapier

As we've seen, a robust onboarding process can lead to growth. App-connecting tool Zapier showed users which platforms they could connect using the program and allowed them to request new platforms. By knowing which platforms their customers use, the company could increase its audience immediately.

#31 Wistia

This company used a growth hack popular with programs embedded into other sites. By providing a link at the bottom saying "powered by Wistia" (a brand affinity marketing software), visitors to that website will want to see what the company does.

#32 Pinterest

This is another "invite-only" example of growth hacking. When it first started, users of Pinterest had to be invited to join, creating an aura of exclusivity. Once you entered, you were encouraged to invite others so that you could share your content (images and videos) with them.

#33 Shopify

In many cases, offering your service for free is an excellent way to encourage people to sign up. Shopify provides a 14-day trial, which is more than enough for small businesses to see how they can use the site to sell online. Once the trial is finished, most users are more than happy to keep their stores open (and pay for the privilege).

#34 Proven

Employees can be your most valuable resource. Proven (a content marketing platform) had a competition among its staff to improve and promote any content that wasn't performing well. The result was more traction for content, and all without spending any money.

#35 WPEngine

Incentivizing references is an excellent growth hacking strategy. WPEngines (a WordPress hosting service provider) gives users $200 for any referrals who use the program.

#36 RJMetrics

Giveaways are another way to build buzz around your company. RJMetrics (ecommerce analytics service) held a social media contest with a dozen cupcakes as the prize. Since everyone loves cupcakes, the contest went viral, and the cost was minimal.

#37 Invision

Like HubSpot, Invision's plan was to create a tool that developers would want to use. In this case, it would allow programmers to test non-functioning sites to see how they would work. In exchange, Invision would create a detailed report. Providing such a useful service led to significant traction for the company.

#38 Slack

Here is another case of providing an excellent service that solves a problem. Poor communication among executive team members was the issue and Slack was the solution. A "freemium" version of the product allowed for rapid expansion. Now the company has over nine million active users.

#39 Poo Pourri

Like Dollar Shave Club, Poo Pourri, which produces fragrant sprays for toilets, created a video ad that went viral. Creating content that people want to share is an excellent way to boost your online profile and get your business trending on social media.

#40 ShopStyle

Synergy is another way to hack your way to growth and ShopStyle is a perfect example. The basis for this site is to help users find and match clothing, then connect them to an online retailer. Stores get more traffic and ShopStyle gets more advertising as these retailers (and fashion bloggers) spread the word.

#41 Buzzfeed

Content creation is the basis for many of these growth hacks. Buzzfeed, an Internet media company focused on breaking news, has been able to capture that perfectly. By creating and curating content that will go viral, the company can permeate the online marketplace. Sometimes, all it takes is a catchy headline and a few juicy quizzes to become popular.

#42 TripAdvisor

These days, online reviews are becoming more necessary than ever. TripAdvisor already had a killer SEO (search engine optimization) marketing strategy, but hacked its way to growth by encouraging hotels to post badges on their own websites showing they were reviewed highly by TripAdvisor members. These badges linked to the TripAdvisor site, which increased traffic and brand awareness.

#43 Hotel Tonight

Part of growth hacking is refining your product to meet user needs. Hotel Tonight fcosued on amazing last-minute deals at top-rated hotels. As the experience gets better, growth follows organically. The more users get better deals the more they come back and refer others.

#44 Tinder

Gamifying an experience is a useful way to make it more engaging and fun. Tinder has succeeded where other apps have failed thanks to its "swipe right" ease of use. By making finding a match like a game of "hot or not," users feel they have more control over their matches.

#45 Moonpig

Moonpig is an online personalized cards and unique gift ideas platform in the UK. The company's viral marketing campaign based on a catchy jingle helped them take-off. Sometimes, the oldest tricks are still the best ones.

#46 Pokemon Go

2016 was the year of Pokemon, as this app took the world by storm and became a sensation. Interestingly, Pokemon Go did this without much advertising. The hack utilized the popularity of the original games, as well as the novelty of augmented reality. Free downloads also helped boost engagement.

#47 Zappos

When e-commerce was still new, clothing and shoes were not quick to catch on because those are items that people like to try on first. Zappos addressed this issue with a "no-questions-asked" return policy, which removed the risk and encouraged shoppers to buy. Oddly enough, those who return the most are the best customers.

#48 Firebox

This e-commerce company leveraged the marketing appeal of affiliate advertising (referral sales based on customized links). Affiliate marketing is a valuable resource because affiliates get paid a commission, so the model is self-funding. Firebox tapped into three affiliate networks, leading to massive growth in a short period.

#49 eBay

Buying and selling items online has always been a risky proposition, especially when the people handling the transactions are unknown. eBay created trust with its customers by including user reviews and escrow protection for buyers.

#50 Kickstarter

Synergy can help propel a company to success. In Kickstarter's case, the hack was tapping into the creative market. Creators had to promote the site to try and get funding for their new projects. Once people — both creators and investors — saw how easy it was, the site exploded in popularity. Today, it's the number one crowdfunding website. (Crowdfunding supports projects that raise small amounts of money from many people via the Internet.)

Summary

In this chapter, we looked at 50 proven growth hacks as inspirations. These examples should help stimulate ideas to implement as your own innovative growth hacks. When looking at these proven techniques consider these approaches.

1. Straightforward copy, but carefully.
2. Copy, but adjust for improvements.
3. Combine some of them and implement.
4. Combinations that trigger something completely new.

CHAPTER NOTES

CHAPTER NOTES

Bonus Chapter C:
88 Tools to Get You Started

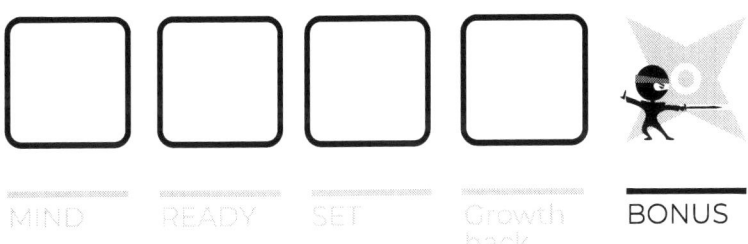

MIND   READY   SET   Growth hack   **BONUS**

In Chapter 2 we looked at how to make the most of the ever-expanding toolkit available to growth hackers. In this bonus chapter, you'll find an extensive list of growth hacking tools, categorized by function. As discussed in Chapter 2, you won't need them all — nor will all of them be suitable for your business. Focus on those that will help you implement your specific ideas from the last chapter, and don't get bogged down in new tool fatigue.

Social Media

Social media tools enable your outreach to fill the top of your funnel — you gain the most visibility and bring in the right type of customers while building the right type of image that best servers your brand. This approach also includes focuses on customer-servicing support.

1. **Click to Tweet** allows you to embed a link that allows users to click on a quote to tweet it on their profiles. *Growth Hack:* A strong presence on social media helps build buzz around your startup.

2. **Pay With a Tweet** incentivizes people to tweet about your product or company with a free ebook or download. *Growth Hack:* By creating strong incentives, you can get substantial Twitter coverage about your brand in a short period.

3. **Colibri.io** allows you to find out what your audience is talking about on social media and insert yourself into the conversation. *Growth Hack:* Gain more traction on social media with targeted messages and engagement.

4. **Twilighter** enables users to highlight any part of your content and post it to Twitter. *Growth Hack:* Get your followers to promote you by making it easy to do so.

5. **YouTube** allows you to create videos and build a subscriber base. *Growth Hack:* Video marketing is always a win, and you can lead people back to your YouTube channel through embeds.

6. **Mention** will show you when and where users are mentioning your business on social media. *Growth Hack:* As your online presence improves, you can join in on these conversations and nurture leads more efficiently.

7. **BuzzSumo** lets you find local influencers online. *Growth Hack:* Leverage influencers' followers to boost your online presence and get more leads.

8. **Po.st** lets people post to social media from your site and allows you to track the results. *Growth Hack:* See how people are sharing your content to social media and then follow up accordingly to boost your online presence.

9. **Post Planner** shows you what your users will see before you post and allows you to automate social media posts. *Growth Hack:* Get into the mindset of your leads and post at the right times to gain more engagement on social media.

10. **Buffer** allows you to manage social media accounts across platforms and integrate them efficiently. *Growth Hack:* Stop wasting time by posting the same content to multiple sites.
11. **Jooicer** enables you to target qualified Twitter users based on user data. *Growth Hack:* Build a better following that will not only buy your product but also refer it to others.

Advertising and SEO

These tools enable you to boost your outreach by getting paid and unpaid traffic to your business. This means also targeting the right customers with the right offering within the right context. Advertising and SEO (search engine optimization) play a vital role in aligning the customer, message, and offering effectively.

12. **Outbrain** allows you to piggyback on the high traffic of news sites like CNN by getting ads posted to their home pages. *Growth Hack:* High visibility of your brand can increase traffic substantially and quickly.
13. **MixRank** uses a database of user data to find out where to target your next ad. *Growth Hack:* Targeted ads have more impact on leads, making them want to sign up.
14. **AdRoll** is great for startups that use paid promotion because you can track who comes to your site through these ads. *Growth Hack:* Knowing how someone found your site enables you to target them more effectively with a compelling CTA.
15. **JustReachOut** allows you to connect with journalists looking for quotes for their next article or story. *Growth Hack:* Boost your online presence and become an authority in your industry.

16. **Snip.ly** enables you to create ads that pop up when people read links you've shared. *Growth Hack:* Customize these ads so that they're related to the link in order to drive more traffic to your site.

17. **CoSchedule Headline Analyzer** is a great way to assess how your headlines will perform. *Growth Hack:* Sometimes, all it takes is changing the wording of a headline to get more clicks and gain more traction with your content.

18. **Ahrefs** tracks mentions and backlinks to your site. It also analyzes how you compare to your competition. *Growth Hack:* Good SEO is all about building links; this tool can help you make sure you're maximizing your efforts. It can also help you create a more effective network to find new leads.

19. **AdEspresso** helps you to create more compelling Facebook ads. *Growth Hack:* Better ads help you get more leads. This tool is beneficial if you don't have experienced marketers on your team yet.

20. **Masskom** lets you gamify the selling process for your sales staff. *Growth Hack:* Motivated salespeople boost revenue quickly. Gamifying the process makes it easier to turn low sales into higher ones.

21. **Outreach Plus** allows you to create a comprehensive outreach campaign to cultivate more qualified leads. *Growth Hack:* Make sure that the people visiting your web pages are interested in what you have to offer so that you can convert them more easily.

22. **SEO Quake** creates parameters for your SEO marketing and shows you how you're performing. *Growth Hack:* This tool can help you make the most from your SEO campaign in a shorter time.

Email Marketing

Email marketing tools enable you to automate your communications by optimizing messaging, design, timing, and call-to-action. Email has been the most consistent source for the highest returns as a tool in digital marketing; it outperforms many newer methods like social media. It still works and will continue to do so. Its solid and automation tools help you boost your ability to better communicate with existing and potential customers.

23. **Constant Contact** helps you to manage even the largest list of email subscribers. You can also receive training to help you further. *Growth Hack:* Email marketing is still a viable method of promoting your brand. Use it wisely.

24. **MailChimp** makes it easy to create new email campaigns and offers extensive analytical tools. *Growth Hack:* Target your subscribers with unique email content geared toward their interests.

25. **Maitre** builds a waiting list for your email subscribers and makes them vie for first place. *Growth Hack:* We've seen what happens when people have to compete for a top spot; take advantage of users' competitive nature.

26. **AWeber** is one of the oldest and simplest email marketing management tools. *Growth Hack:* Build custom templates that will encourage subscribers to follow up on an offer.

27. **List Builder 3** helps you create a pop up that encourages site visitors to subscribe to your email list. *Growth Hack:* You can control when and how the pop up engages with the user, making it more effective.

28. **Mailgun** analyzes your email subscribers and gives you verification that email addresses are correct. *Growth Hack:* Make sure that your email marketing is as compelling as possible and stop missing out on leads because users misspelled their email addresses.

29. **Verio** helps you to understand your email subscribers by gaining insight into their interests. *Growth Hack:* You can come up with a much more effective email marketing campaign when you know what will get people to open your message.

30. **Customer.io** allows you to create customized messages for your customers and automate when they're sent. *Growth Hack:* Nurture your customers and build loyalty by creating personalized messages and sending them consistently.

31. **SendGrid** is a massive email marketing tool that offers a variety of systems to make it easy to manage contacts and subscriber lists. *Growth Hack:* Scaling up is easy with this software, ensuring your business scales as you grow with their solution.

32. **Sendwithus** creates a more effective drip campaign with customized transactional emails. *Growth Hack:* Automating an email campaign can lead to more conversions.

33. **Klaviyo** connects your email management tool with your customer analytics. *Growth Hack:* Build synergy between analysis tools and email marketing so that you can be more efficient in reaching and connecting with your subscribers.

34. **Emma** creates emails based on user behavior. *Growth Hack:* Emailing a user at the right time can increase engagement and build a better subscriber base.

35. **Cloud Sponge** lets you create a larger subscriber network by finding the contacts of your current user base. *Growth Hack:* Increase your connections exponentially and develop a rapid referral program.

Automation Tools

These types of tools enable you to use fewer resources, including your time to supercharge revenue by optimizing routine activities while streamlining non-routine activities. Good automation tools help you focus on what counts most.

36. **Marketo** integrates all of your marketing tools into one place. *Growth Hack:* By automating your marketing process, you can save time, money, and energy, making your startup even leaner.
37. **Zapier** creates automated tools that integrate multiple platforms together. *Growth Hack:* Zapier connects different accounts so that integration is smoother and you can work more efficiently.
38. **SketchDeck** allows you to connect with a team of designers who will create compelling content for you. *Growth Hack:* Leverage a team of professional creatives to generate content that will get noticed and shared faster.

Testing and Analytics

In order to ensure you optimize your ability to detect the best way to reach customers, testing and analytics help you focus on where to place more resources that give you a better outcome. Good testing and analytics help you detect opportunities or risks you have not seen and show you how to best tap into them.

39. **Pingdom** tests the speed of your website so that you can make it faster if necessary. *Growth Hack:* If your site is slow, you'll lose potential leads.
40. **GeckoBoard** analyzes all your metrics in one easy-to-read dashboard. *Growth Hack:* Analysis allows you to refine your approach and focus on what works the best.

41. **Google Analytics** allows you to leverage the massive amount of data that Google can produce about your SEO results. *Growth Hack:* If you can improve your SEO ranking, you can boost your online presence and site traffic faster.

42. **Consumer Barometer** enables you to access valuable data about users from around the world. *Growth Hack:* Understanding leads coming from different regions allows you to target them more efficiently.

43. **Five Second Test** gives you feedback on what sticks out from your site in five seconds. *Growth Hack:* Make sure that your leads will convert with a site that is immediately captivating.

44. **Session Cam** helps you to watch your customers through their webcam footage when they visit your site. *Growth Hack:* Make sure that your page layout and calls-to-action (CTAs) are having their intended effect and adjust accordingly.

45. **Amplitude** breaks down your data and statistics by tying them to real people. *Growth Hack:* Stop looking at numbers and start viewing your leads as real users. Doing this will allow you to develop a stronger conversion campaign.

46. **CrazyEgg** analyzes how users interact with your site; it uses heatmaps as visual representation of user behavior and other tools. *Growth Hack:* Find out how to make your site more compelling to convert more leads into customers.

47. **Totango** analyzes your site visitors by ranking them based on how they interact with your website. *Growth Hack:* Focus your attention on the leads that matter and make your conversion process smoother.

48. **KingSumo** lets you test and find the best headline that will get clicks. *Growth Hack:* This tool generates the headline for you, saving you time and energy.

49. **Olark** enables you to build prompts into your site that ensure visitors feel seen and recognized. It also allows you to analyze their behavior on your pages. *Growth Hack:* Understand what your leads value most about your site and refine it as much as possible.

50. **Qualaroo** gives you valuable insights into your leads and site visitors. *Growth Hack:* Understanding your visitors helps you customize content and make more effective CTAs.

51. **SEMRush** will analyze your site and show you what keywords are trending among your competition. *Growth Hack:* Optimize your website more efficiently and find out what's working for your competitors so that you can capitalize on the same keywords.

52. **Optimizely** runs A/B tests of your website to discover which changes have the most impact. *Growth Hack:* Focus your attention on a layout that works, rather than wasting time on one that doesn't.

53. **ClickTale** gives you customized insight into your site visitors and helps you understand how they interact with your pages. *Growth Hack:* When combined with A/B testing, you can hack your way to a more conversion-friendly site.

54. **Coastics** gives you customized emails from Google Analytics without logging into your account. *Growth Hack:* Make it easier to get insight from Google, saving more time in the process.

55. **Swagger.io** helps you to build a more effective API (communications protocol that connect software programs together) by sharing it with a network of developers. *Growth Hack:* Don't hire more developers to your team — use Swagger.io instead. Refine your API so that it's better and more productive than ever.

56. **Segment** looks for trends in your customer data. *Growth Hack:* Gain valuable insight into your lead data so that you can adjust your content and site accordingly to get more conversions.

57. **KISSMetrics** analyzes data from the lifecycle of your leads and conversions. *Growth Hack:* The data collected by KISSMetrics is more comprehensive than other analytical tools, allowing you to adjust your marketing more precisely.

58. **Apptimize** allows mobile app builders to optimize it with A/B tests and other tools. *Growth Hack:* Make sure that your app appeals to its users by testing and refining it as much as possible.

59. **UserTesting** sends your website to a user panel to give you valuable insight. *Growth Hack:* Get data from qualified users who know what to look for and how to relay the information to you.

60. **BareMetrics** gives you analytics for your email subscriptions. *Growth Hack:* Knowing how well your email marketing is going can help you course correct and ensure better returns on your investment.

61. **HotJar** provides feedback from customers in the form of surveys and heatmaps. *Growth Hack:* Get insight from your users themselves so that you know what to change (if necessary).

62. **Visual Website Optimizer** helps you to conduct A/B Tests on your website. *Growth Hack:* See how people respond to the visual elements of your site to make it more impactful.

63. **Chart Mogul** gives you analytics and metrics for your subscriber lists in an easy-to-use dashboard. *Growth Hack:* Integrate analysis with email marketing to increase conversions and retention.

64. **Growth Report** gives you a customized report analyzing how well your marketing is doing. *Growth Hack:* Use this report to make sure that your hacks are operating according to plan.

65. **Majestic** shows you how different sites are connected. *Growth Hack:* Compare your backlinks to your competitors to see where you rank.

Conversions and Engagement

Conversion and engagement tools are designed to boost your revenue by ensuring the alignment of your message and offering the best alignment with target customers. They are vital in detecting opportunities and risks you don't see, things emerging, and things that work and do not work so you can focus on what best works to generate more revenue.

66. **OptinMonster** allows you to create CTAs (calls-to-action) and opt-in forms for your website or landing page. *Growth Hack:* Compelling CTAs have a variety of uses, from encouraging downloads to building a network of subscribers.

67. **ManyChat** creates chatbots that integrate with Facebook's Messenger app. *Growth Hack:* Users want to work with companies that listen. A robot automatically saves time and resources by engaging immediately so that leads don't lose interest.

68. **Nimble** is a customer relationship management (CRM) tool that manages contacts across different channels. *Growth Hack:* If you want to convert leads, you need to nurture them over time. Also, don't lose track of leads and lose their business.

69. **LeadPages** helps you to create compelling landing pages with different templates and creation tools. *Growth Hack:* A landing page is vital in getting leads to convert to sales. LeadPages makes it easy to do.

70. **MixPanel** allows you to build customer funnels and see how leads interact with each stage of it. *Growth Hack:* Find out where leads are bouncing the most and adjust your funnel accordingly to get more conversions.

71. **Hello Bar** enables you to build a call-to-action (CTA) bar into your website. *Growth Hack:* This bar is fully customizable, and it can be integrated into different landing pages for better results.

72. **Referral Candy** encourages referrals by offering incentives for customers (online storefronts only). *Growth Hack:* Building a reliable referral program ensures that your customers become brand ambassadors.

73. **UserLane** gamifies the onboarding process for users new to your software or system. *Growth Hack:* A rewarding onboarding process leads to better retention, and it ensures that users get more value from your app or software.

74. **HubSpot** is another CRM tool that helps you manage your leads and customers. *Growth Hack:* Not only manage your customers, but also create content that will attract new ones more efficiently.

75. **Bounce Exchange** creates a calls-to-action (CTAs) that pops up when someone is about to leave your site. *Growth Hack:* Convert more leads when you have multiple CTAs on your page.

76. **Unbounce** helps you to build calls-to-action (CTAs) and see how well they work using Unbounce's analytics. *Growth Hack:* Refining your CTAs will make them more effective over time.

77. **InfusionSoft** is a fully integrated CRM program. *Growth Hack:* Although this software does have a learning curve, it's one of the most capable CRM programs available.

78. **Quora** allows you to set up an account and start answering questions related to your industry. *Growth Hack:* Establish your startup as an authority in the field and generate leads accordingly.

79. **Zoom** allows you to create webinars that will encourage users to engage with your brand. *Growth Hack:* Although webinars don't work for all businesses, they provide an excellent way to establish authority in your industry.

80. **Typeform** can create quizzes that will drive customer engagement and keep people coming back for more. *Growth Hack:* Make your brand more entertaining

and encourage long-term engagement that will build sales and referrals.

81. **PollDaddy** creates polls that you can send to your subscribers. *Growth Hack:* Not only will the polls offer insight into your customers, but it helps them stay engaged with your brand.

82. **Branch** allows you to create a branded link that goes directly to a page on your website (not a landing page). *Growth Hack:* If you want to generate sales, make a link that will send people to a product page or something similar. These links can be highly valuable when implemented creatively.

83. **Appcues** makes the onboarding process simpler and easier for new users. *Growth Hack:* When onboarding is enjoyable, people are much more likely to stick with the product and recommend it to others.

84. **Sonar** lets your customers text you with questions or comments. *Growth Hack:* Stand above the competition with a text-based communication system. More people prefer to text businesses these days, so accommodate your users.

85. **Wistia** allows you to embed videos into your pages. *Growth Hack:* As we mentioned, video marketing is a great way to facilitate engagement with your leads.

86. **OptiMonk** enables you to track when users enter and leave a page and create a CTA accordingly. *Growth Hack:* Combine analytics with CTA creation to get the best of both worlds.

87. **FOMO** shares customer interactions to showcase how popular your pages are. *Growth Hack:* Customize this widget and get leverage that will encourage people to find out more about what you have to offer.

88. **Extole** finds people who are recommending your product already and connects with them. *Growth Hack:* Build a reliable referral program without having to resort to guesswork.

Summary

In this chapter, we have looked at 88 tools categorized into their purpose as a starting point to source and tools for growth hacking. Not all tools are perfect, but they are now cheaper and even free in some cases and easy to use. This greatly lowers the risks associated with these tools. The types of tools we have covered are:

1. Social Media
2. Advertising and SEO
3. Email Marketing
4. Automation Tools
5. Testing and Analytics
6. Conversions and Engagement

No matter what tool you use, eventually you will have to create your own once you maximize these off the shelf solution. Remember these solutions can last you a while and bring quite a bit of results; they are not to be underestimated in any way or shape. Booking.com conducts 1,000 tests a day with their own tools that took them years to develop, but these tools do exactly what the company needs.

CHAPTER NOTES

CHAPTER NOTES

Bonus Chapter D: Glossary

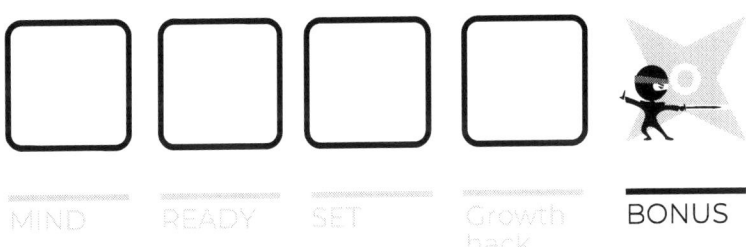

MIND   READY   SET   Growth hack   **BONUS**

API (application programming interface) — a set of functions and procedures allowing the creation of applications that access the features or data of an operating system, application, or other service

Automation — the method or system of controlling a process by automatic means, reducing human intervention to a minimum

Bot — also known as a robot, an autonomous program (used especially on the Internet) that can interact with systems or users

Chatbot — a computer program designed to simulate conversation with human users, especially over the Internet

Crowdfunding — the practice of funding a project or venture by raising money from a large number of people who each contribute a relatively small amount, typically via the Internet

CTA (call to action) — a statement designed to get an immediate response from the person reading or hearing it to respond through actions

CTR (click through rate) — the ratio of users who click on a specific link to the number of total users who view a page, email, or advertisement

Customer journey — the complete sum of experiences that customers go through when interacting with your company and brand

CRM (customer relationship management) — an approach to manage interactions with current and potential customers by user data analysis to improve business to retention customers and ultimately driving sales growth

Customer pain point — a specific problem your customers are facing that need to be solved more urgently than others, as they want to get rid of the pain

Drip marketing — a communication strategy that sends pre-written messages to customers, nurturing the relationship with customers with compelling content and eventually leading them to sales

Gamification — the application of game playing (e.g., point scoring, competition with others, rules of play) to other activities, typically as a technique to encourage engagement with a product or service

Growth hacking —a shortcut to growth. It's about finding the most effective methods for growing your business in the shortest amount of time

Heatmaps — a representation of data in the form of a map or diagram in which data values are represented as colors, typically used to understand user behavior on a website

Landing page — a single web page that appears in response to clicking from a search engine or advertisement with a single focused proposition to improve sales

Onboarding — a process of welcoming new customers, addressing their questions and concerns, and ensuring they understand the services available to them and how to use them effectively

SaaS (Software as a service) — a method of software delivery and licensing in which software is accessed online via a subscription, rather than bought and installed on individual computers.

Scalability and scaling — the capacity to change in size with ease to ensure continuity of your business operations as you grow

SEO (search engine optimization) — the process that organizations go through to help make sure that their website ranks high in the search engines for relevant keywords and phrases

CONCLUSION

Congratulations, you are ready, set, and able to growth hack. This book is designed to help you walk to through the basics of the process and build on them. Using the exercises in the book, you can conduct your first phase of growth hacks. Use them and expand on them using them for your next round of growth hacks.

81% of organizations have a growth problem whereas only 8% of them actively tackle their growth issues directly. Often, cultiire and bumaticracy get directly in the way of forming a growth mindset across the whole organization that enables growth.

Incremental growth keeps most organizations comfortable, but that comfort is a blind spot — growth isn't comfortable by nature. This source of discomfort is where real growth comes from. Discomfort doesn't mean being in pain all the time, but further toning your organization's growth muscles.

ABOUT THE AUTHOR

Nader Sabry is a keynote speaker, strategist, innovator, and entrepreneur as well as a leading voice in innovation, space technology, government, and health/wellness. He is a passionate advocate for inspiring the youth to embrace science and technology, through the Get2space.com initiative in partnership with the US Space Foundation.

Sabry has directly raised US $20 million in venture capital, indirectly $100 million for startups he has advised or cofounded, and $3 billion in foreign direct investment. He was the 43rd person in history to be NASA Space Technology certified, has served as a judge for the US Space Foundation's Space Technology Hall of Fame, is a top-50 writer globally on medium.com, has been ranked one of the top 13 innovators in the MENA region making a difference by Step Conference, and was featured by A.T. Kearney as one of their top alumni.

Sabry is the former CEO and Founder of TIMEZ5 Global Inc.; a Canadian space technology certified company by NASA's Space Foundation, and a GIES Innovation award winner from His Highness Sheikh Mohammed Bin Rashid Al Maktoum. TIMEZ5 was founded 2012 after five years of R&D selling in 37 countries; it has been recommended by healthcare professionals globally.

Prior to TIMEZ5 Global, Sabry was head of innovation and thought leadership at A.T. Kearney, chief strategist for The Dubai Department of Economic Development, and director of strategy for the Dubai Foreign Investment Office. He has also advised several governments and Fortune 1000 companies.

Sabry contributes to innovation globally as a published author, speaker, and lecturer, and as the former chairman of the Institute for Strategy Complexity Management forum. Additionally, he has been featured in **Time Magazine, Huffington Post, Financial times – merger markets, MIT Technology Review, and NASA's premier publication Spinoff**.

As a University of Cambridge graduate, Sabry attained his postgraduate education in business administration and holds an MBA, BComm, and business diploma.

Sabry's work has been described as, "He is the guy you don't want your competition to hire...."

Book website

www.ReadySetGrowthHack.com

Author website

www.nadersabry.com

Printed in Great Britain
by Amazon

74727769R00124